• MIKE PIAZZA • AL LOPEZ • GIL HODGES • DOLPH
Y • JACKIE ROBINSON • JIM GILLIAM •
RUSSELL • MAURY WILLS • LEO DUROCHER • LONNY
E LAVAGETTO • JOE MEDWICK • TOMMY DAVIS • ZACK
WILLIE DAVIS • BRETT BUTLER • RICK MONDAY • MAX
• BABE HERMAN • FRANK HOWARD • DON DRYSDALE
ES • CARL ERSKINE • SANDY KOUFAX • PREACHER
OMMY JOHN • ERIC GAGNE • CLEM LABINE • RON
DRESSEN • WALTER ALSTON • TOMMY LASORDA •
RO • STEVE YEAGER • MIKE PIAZZA • AL LOPEZ • GIL
• EDDIE MURRAY • JACKIE ROBINSON • JIM GILLIAM •
WEE REESE • BILL RUSSELL • MAURY WILLS • LEO
X • RON CEY • COOKIE LAVAGETTO • JOE MEDWICK •
SON • PETE REISER • WILLIE DAVIS • BRETT BUTLER •
E SMITH • DIXIE WALKER • BABE HERMAN • FRANK
VANCE • BURLEIGH GRIMES • CARL ERSKINE • SANDY
O VALENZUELA • TOMMY JOHN • ERIC GAGNE • CLEM
K • CHARLIE DRESSEN • WALTER ALSTON • TOMMY
HN ROSEBORO • STEVE YEAGER • MIKE PIAZZA • AL

FEW AND CHOSEN

Defining Dodgers Greatness across the Eras

Duke Snider

with Phil Pepe

TRIUMPH
BOOKS

CHICAGO

Library of Congress Cataloging-in-Publication Data

Snider, Duke, 1926–
    Few and chosen : defining Dodgers greatness across the eras / Duke Snider with Phil Pepe.
        p. cm.
    Includes index.
    ISBN-13: 978-1-57243-805-7
    ISBN-10: 1-57243-805-3
    1. Los Angeles Dodgers (Baseball team)—History. 2. Brooklyn Dodgers (Baseball team)—History. 3. Baseball players—Rating of. I. Pepe, Phil. II. Title.

GV875.L6S65 2006
796.357′640979494—dc22

                                                                                    2005052922

This book is available in quantity at special discounts for your group or organization. For further information, contact:

Triumph Books
542 South Dearborn Street
Suite 750
Chicago, Illinois 60605
(312) 939-3330
Fax (312) 663-3557

Printed in U.S.A.
ISBN-13: 978-1-57243-805-7
ISBN-10: 1-57243-805-3
Design by Nick Panos; page production by Patricia Frey
All photos courtesy of AP/Wide World Photos unless indicated otherwise.

Contents

Foreword

I looked high and low at my pal Duke Snider's choices for the top five Dodgers of all time at each position, and I couldn't find my name anywhere. You know why I couldn't find my name? Because it's not there. And it shouldn't be. How could you put a lifetime .235 hitter like me on a team with guys like Arky Vaughan, Billy Herman, Pee Wee Reese, Maury Wills, Jim Gilliam, Ron Cey, and Jackie Robinson?

Don't get me wrong. I'm not complaining. What have I got to complain about? I consider myself a very lucky guy. For more than 50 consecutive years I have collected a paycheck for doing the only thing I know: playing, managing, and coaching the game I love, the greatest game ever invented—baseball.

Who has had it better than I have? I have had a wonderful baseball life. I played alongside great players: Hall of Famers Jackie Robinson, Pee Wee Reese, Roy Campanella, and Duke Snider in Brooklyn; Sandy Koufax and Don Drysdale in Los Angeles; Ernie Banks and Billy Williams in Chicago; Richie Ashburn in New York; and Frank Robinson in Cincinnati. I played for legendary managers: Walter Alston with the Dodgers, Casey Stengel with the Mets, Fred Hutchinson with the Reds, and Gil Hodges with the Senators.

I managed Hall of Famers Carl Yastrzemski and Carlton Fisk in Boston, Fergie Jenkins in Texas, and Ryne Sandberg in Chicago. And I sat alongside Joe Torre as bench coach of the Yankees when we won four World Series in six years.

And I was a member of the team that won Brooklyn's only World Series in 1955.

I have been with a lot of different teams during my 50-plus years in baseball, but my roots are with the Dodgers in Brooklyn. I suppose I will always think of myself as a Dodger.

I came up through the Dodgers organization, joined them in Brooklyn in 1954, and stayed with them through 1959 in Los Angeles. When I got to Brooklyn, I was just a kid filled with hope and overflowing with confidence. I thought I was a pretty good ballplayer. I was going to be the guy who would bump Reese off shortstop. A lot of guys had tried—a couple dozen, actually—but I thought I was going to be the one to succeed. But Pee Wee buried me like he buried all of the rest.

I was frustrated in Brooklyn because I wanted to play, but the truth is I wasn't good enough to play in that lineup. Who was I going to replace? Pee Wee at shortstop? Jackie Robinson at second base? Billy Cox at third?

I sometimes thought that if there had not been a Pee Wee Reese, I might have been the shortstop on that club. But there was a Pee Wee, and he buried all the shortstops that came along. I felt I could play on many clubs, and I asked to be traded. But when I finally did get traded to the Cubs in 1960, it hurt.

I loved being a Dodger. I enjoyed playing on such great teams with such great guys. We were a close-knit group. There were about five or six of us who loved to go to the horse track, and we'd often go in a group: me, Duke, Pee Wee, Gil Hodges, and Jackie Robinson. Probably the best thing about my Dodgers days was the friendships I made, some of which are still going more than 50 years later.

I first met Duke Snider in Vero Beach, Florida, at spring training in 1953. We became friends right away, and we're still close friends today. Duke was a special player. He was great. He wasn't just a home-run hitter. He could throw and he could field. He had great hands. I never saw Duke drop a fly ball. Not once. And he could run. He was a lot like Stan Musial. He would hit a ground ball to deep short and beat it out. I've seen him beat out bunts for base hits with his speed.

At the time New York had three great center fielders: Mickey Mantle with the Yankees, Willie Mays with the Giants, and Duke. I have always believed that Snider never got the credit he deserved for his defense because he wasn't playing in the right ballpark. Mantle had Yankee Stadium and Mays had the Polo Grounds, both stadiums with cavernous center fields so the ballplayers could run all day and make spectacular running catches. Duke had the ability to do that, but Ebbets Field had such a small center field that he'd go four steps and be at the wall. If you had put Snider in Yankee Stadium or the Polo Grounds, he would have made those spectacular running catches, and he would have earned a reputation for his defense just like Mantle, Mays, and Joe DiMaggio did.

Duke didn't pick me for his all-time Dodgers team, but I can tell you this: if I were to pick my all-time Dodgers team, Duke Snider would certainly be on it.

More important, if I were to list my closest friends, Duke would be on that list too—at the top!

—Don Zimmer

Preface

Ican barely remember a time when baseball was not a part of my life, and where and when I spent my youth—the borough of Brooklyn in the forties—baseball meant the Dodgers. The *Brooklyn Dodgers!* That was before Walter O'Malley ripped out a huge chunk of my heart by moving the team almost a continent away to Los Angeles.

I was six years old when I first became aware of the wonderful game called baseball that would grip me for a lifetime, and of the Dodgers, who were inescapable in that time and place. All around me were Dodgers fans—aunts and uncles, cousins and friends—and I simply fell in with the crowd. In later years it would be called "bonding."

My first baseball memory is listening to my elders curse the fate of their beloved, snakebitten Dodgers after the fourth game of the 1941 World Series against the Yankees. Something about a catcher named Mickey Owen dropping a third strike that enabled a Yankee named Tommy Henrich to reach first base safely and pave the way for those damn Yankees to stage a game-winning, back-breaking, ninth-inning rally.

My aunts and uncles and cousins and friends were devastated by the day's events, not to mention frustrated and angry; so I was devastated, frustrated, and angry too, although I really didn't understand what all the fuss was about.

A year later my aunt and uncle took me to my first game, the Dodgers versus the Giants. I remember to this day, six decades later, the excitement and exhilaration I felt as I emerged from the subway and walked past the Bond Bread sign, past the botanical gardens of Prospect Park. I remember turning a corner and my little boy's heart leaping for joy as there, rising before me, was the Ebbets Field rotunda.

My eyes opened as wide as banjos when we arrived at our seats. I tried to take it all in, from the enormous screen in right field that seemed to rise to the sky, to the Abe Stark sign beneath that screen—Hit Sign, Win Suit—to the vast expanse of carefully manicured grass and dirt, to the white chalk lines marking the foul lines and the batter's box, to the men in white uniforms with the blue script *Dodgers* across their chests—my heroes come to life.

The grass was the greenest green and the uniforms the whitest white I had ever seen.

I listened to the discordant sounds of the Brooklyn Sym-phony, oompah-pahing a visiting player all the way back to the dugout after he struck out, and then exploding with a crash of cymbals and drums when that player plopped himself down on the bench. I heard a shrill voice shrieking, "Cook-ie!" whenever Cookie Lavagetto appeared.

I cheered wildly when Dolph Camilli belted one over the right-field wall, unable to fathom how anyone could hit a baseball that far, and when Billy Herman drilled a line-drive double into the right-field corner. And I left this Shangri-la of my youth happy; I had seen the Dodgers, *my* Dodgers, defeat the hated Giants. I was hooked for life!

In the years that followed, my love affair with baseball, with the Dodgers, flourished. I was consumed by the game, the team. I cajoled my aunt into teaching me long division before I learned it in school so I could compute batting averages. I avidly followed my Dodgers on the radio, through the syrupy sweet, Southern tones of Red Barber. There were no portable radios in those days, but none were needed in my neighborhood. One had only to stroll through the streets on warm summer days to follow the progress of the Dodgers from radio broadcasts pouring out of the open windows of almost every home.

On summer mornings I would wake early and rush around to the corner candy store to buy a newspaper and read about the previous day's game in the *New York Daily News*' stories by Dick Young, who quickly became my favorite sportswriter and, years later, my mentor and colleague.

My favorite player in my youth, to whom I was no doubt attracted by his nickname, was "Pee Wee" Reese. I fantasized about someday replacing him as Dodgers shortstop. I proudly informed my friends that Reese's real first name was Harold but that everybody called him Pee Wee, a name he picked up—I learned from Dick Young—because as a boy he was a marble champion in his native Louisville, Kentucky, wherever that was.

When I was 11 years old, I saw my first no-hitter, pitched by an obscure Dodger named Ed Head, who would win only 26 other games in his major league career. A year later my brother Paul and I went to Ebbets Field to watch the Dodgers play their International League farm team, the Montreal Royals, in an exhibition game prior to the opening of the 1947 season. We watched an African-American infielder play for Montreal, but we were oblivious to the social significance of the event until we read in the next day's newspaper that Jackie Robinson's contract had been purchased by the Dodgers and that he would be their Opening Day first baseman—the first black man to play in a major league game.

The arrival of Robinson would signal a resurgence in Dodgers dominance in the National League following World War II. They won the pennant in 1947 but again lost to the Yankees in the World Series.

To root for the Dodgers was to endure some of the most unspeakable, excruciating disappointments any baseball fan could suffer. Brooklyn was the home office for heartbreak; the Dodgers were the lovable losers, from Mickey Owen's dropped third strike in 1941, to Bobby Thomson's shot heard 'round the world 10 years later, to the utter futility of trying to beat the Yankees in the World Series. Out of that futility was born the "Brooklyn Bum," legendary sports cartoonist Willard Mullin's comical characterization of the Dodgers as a bedraggled, down-and-out, bumbling, lumbering lummox, and the oft-repeated lament that would become the Dodgers' motto: "Wait till next year!"

To root for the Dodgers was to be witness to some of the greatest moments in baseball history: from the major league's longest game, a 26-inning, 1–1 tie between the Dodgers and Boston in 1920 to Johnny Vander Meer's second consecutive no-hitter in 1938; from Bill Bevens' near no-hitter in the 1947 World Series to Don Larsen's perfect game in the 1956 World Series; from Al Gionfriddo's catch of Joe DiMaggio's drive in the 1947 World Series to Sandy Amoros' catch of Yogi Berra's twisting drive in the 1955 World Series; from Reggie Jackson's three home runs in the 1977 World Series to Kirk Gibson's dramatic game-winning, ninth-inning home run off Dennis Eckersley in the 1988 World Series.

To root for the Dodgers was to see some of the game's greatest players: Hall of Famers "Iron Man" Joe McGinnity, Dan Brouthers, Zack Wheat, Max Carey, Dazzy Vance, Burleigh Grimes, Babe Herman, Pee Wee Reese, Roy Campanella, Jackie Robinson, Duke Snider, Don Drysdale, Sandy Koufax, and Don Sutton.

To root for the Dodgers was to follow one of the most storied franchises in baseball history: the winner of 21 pennants, the most by a National League franchise. And to root for the Dodgers was to be witness to a laundry list of baseball firsts. The Dodgers were:

- the first team to have a player hold out for an entire season (pitcher Tom Lovett in 1892);
- the first New York team to broadcast games on the radio (1939);
- the first team to televise a game (August 26, 1939);
- the first major league team to fly to a game (1940);
- the first team to wear batting helmets, that is, bands sewn into players' caps, a rudimentary precursor to today's batting helmet (1941);
- the first team, with the St. Louis Cardinals, to participate in a post-season playoff (1946);
- the first major league team with an African-American player, Jackie Robinson (1947);
- the first team to televise a game in color (August 10, 1951);
- the first major league team—joined by the New York Giants—to play on the West Coast (1958) (Editor's note: It boggles my mind that through the 2005 season, the Dodgers have spent almost as many years in Los Angeles [48] as they did in Brooklyn [68]); and
- the first team to draw more than 3 million fans in a season (1978).

Brooklyn entered the National League in 1890 as the Bridegrooms—so named because a number of its players were married in a short period of time in 1888—and won the pennant their first year in the league. They would go through several name changes: the Superbas, after a popular vaudeville act of the day, "Hanlon's Superbas" (Ned Hanlon was the manager of the Dodgers at the time); the Robins, for their popular manager and co-owner Wilbert Robinson; Trolley Dodgers because dodging trolleys was a familiar occurrence in bustling, pre-1900 Brooklyn; and that name eventually truncated to Dodgers.

Brooklyn was where Casey Stengel, as manager from 1934 to 1936, honed his reputation as a clown by carrying an umbrella to the third-base coach's box, opening it, and holding it over his head in inclement weather, and by doffing his cap for a sparrow to fly from it.

Brooklyn was where the mighty Babe Ruth was last seen in uniform, as a coach in 1938, and where Hall of Famer Sandy Koufax, a native son, made his major league debut.

As a boy, I was so engrossed in the Dodgers that I subscribed to *The Sporting News* and eagerly awaited its weekly delivery, when I would avidly peruse the minor league batting averages to track the progress of future Dodgers, such as Bill Sharman, Bill Antonello, George Shuba, and a young, power-hitting outfielder from California named Edwin Donald Snider, who were playing in such places as Montreal, St. Paul, and Fort Worth.

Snider was called "Duke," and he came with a can't-miss tag, a future star who would move into the middle of the batting order and patrol center field for years. He was a million-dollar baseball player who played for a top salary of $42,000 and for the pure love of the game that, like so many others, gripped him when he was a boy.

Snider debuted with the Dodgers in 1947, two days after Jackie Robinson's first major league game. It would be two more years before Duke took over as the Dodgers' center fielder, where he would remain for 14 distinguished, and mostly spectacular, seasons. In 1949 he batted .292, hit 23 home runs, drove in 92 runs, and helped the Dodgers win another pennant. Alas, once again, they lost to the Yankees in the World Series.

In the fifties Snider was a full-fledged star, carving out a Hall of Fame career, one of three future Hall of Fame center fielders in New York—Willie Mays with the New York Giants in Manhattan, Mickey Mantle with the New York Yankees in the Bronx, and of course, Snider with the Dodgers in Brooklyn.

I joined thousands of others in the raging debate of the day—who is the best center fielder, Willie, Mickey, or the Duke?—arguing my case on street corners, in soda shops, and in classrooms, staunchly supporting my guy, Snider.

I pointed out that in the four-year period from 1954 to 1957, the Duke hit more home runs and drove in more runs than his two New York center-field contemporaries. He also batted over .300 seven times, hit 40 or more home

XIII

runs in a season for five straight years, drove in more than 100 runs in four consecutive years, and is the Dodgers' all-time leader in home runs (389), runs batted in (1,271), and extra-base hits (814).

Years later I would get to know all three New York center fielders. I collaborated on a book with Mantle, and now I have the privilege of collaborating on a book with Snider.

As the player who hit the last home run in Ebbets Field and got the first hit in Dodger Stadium, Snider is uniquely qualified to select his all-time Dodgers team, five players at each position, including the Brooklyn and Los Angeles teams. When his major league career ended, he stayed in the game as a minor league manager, hitting instructor, and broadcaster in Los Angeles and Montreal. Today he resides in Southern California and still follows the Dodgers on television, with occasional visits to Dodger Stadium. As such, he has seen most of the players he selected to his all-time team, and many of them were his teammates.

You will note one glaring omission on Duke's list. Modesty prevents him from selecting himself, but he is clearly the greatest center fielder in Dodgers history and at the top of any list of all-time great Dodgers.

This book is a labor of love for this old Brooklyn boy and Dodgers fan. I am indebted to Duke for this nostalgic journey and for affording me this rare opportunity to revisit my long-ago youth.

—Phil Pepe

Acknowledgments

It has been said that producing a book is like giving birth: you submit a manuscript and, nine months later, out pops a book.

The authors don't know about that. Although they have seven children between them, theirs was only a supporting role in those productions.

One person who does know firsthand about producing a book *and* a child is Triumph Books' former managing editor, Blythe Hurley, who masterfully, skillfully, artfully, and patiently managed the production of four *Few and Chosen* titles, and then went off to produce her own miracle, her first baby.

We thank her for her hard work, her diligence, and her support.

If this was her final act in publishing, she was Bobby Thomson, Bill Mazeroski, and Joe Carter all in one. She hit a walk-off home run. We wish her only the best in her new career: motherhood.

The authors also wish to thank those who generously gave of their time and provided remembrances and insights into old Dodgers, as teammates and opponents: Don Zimmer, Monte Irvin, Tommy John, Marty Marion, Ron Santo, Emil J. "Buzzie" Bavasi, Clyde King, Jim Kaat, Ralph Branca, George "Shotgun" Shuba, Johnny Podres, and Gene Tenace.

Introduction

One day when I was just a kid, I walked in the door and my dad said, "Here comes the Duke." I have no idea where that came from or why he said it. Nobody had ever called me that before, but from that day on Dad kept calling me "Duke," and the name stuck, to my everlasting gratitude.

"Duke" had a nice ring to it. I was born Edwin Donald Snider. The Edwin of Flatbush? How would that sound?

Another thing Dad did when I was very young was make me bat left-handed, even though I did everything else—throw, write, eat—right-handed.

Although he played the game as an amateur, Dad wasn't much of a base-ball player, but he was a huge baseball fan. As a young man, Dad moved to Southern California, where I was born and grew up, but he was raised in Ohio, not far from Cincinnati, and that's where he became a fan. He played a little bit, not a lot, and he didn't have much talent, but he loved the game.

He knew baseball well enough to know that you're a couple steps closer to first base if you bat left-handed, that most of the ballparks are built to favor left-handed hitters, and that there are more right-handed than left-handed pitchers. He obviously didn't know that batting left-handed would stand me in good stead when I got to Brooklyn. I was on a team that was so heavily loaded with right-handed hitters that we rarely saw left-handed pitchers.

Dad passed his love of baseball on to me, and as a kid I was consumed by the game, not only playing it, but also watching it, listening to it on the radio, and reading about it.

I became a Brooklyn Dodgers fan in 1941. I was 14 years old at the time, and the Dodgers had a great team that year. They won the pennant. So, like most kids, I attached myself to a winner. And I was attracted to the Dodgers mainly because of Pee Wee Reese and Pete Reiser. I became a fan of Reese because of his nickname and of Reiser because he led the league in hitting that year, stole home a lot, and did all sorts of exciting things.

I remember listening to the 1941 World Series. The teachers brought radios to school, and we were able to listen to the games in class. I was pulling for the Dodgers mainly because of Reiser and Reese. I used to read about them in *The Sporting News*. There was no major league baseball in California at the time, so *The Sporting News* and the box scores in the daily newspapers were just about all we could get.

The way the Dodgers lost that 1941 World Series to the Yankees—the ball getting by Mickey Owen and all that—only served to make me root for them all the more. I guess I felt sorry for them—I was for the underdog even way back then.

Just about that time I became aware of a young Californian who was the greatest athlete I had ever seen. His name was Jackie Robinson, and he played baseball, football, and basketball and ran track for Pasadena Junior College, the rival of our local school, Compton Junior College.

One day some of my buddies and I went to watch a baseball game between Pasadena and Compton. This fellow Robinson was playing for Pasadena, and all of a sudden, in the middle of the game, we saw him leave the field in his baseball uniform, go over to where a track meet was being held, compete in the broad jump, and then come back to finish the baseball game. That fall I was watching a football game between Pasadena and Compton, and I saw Robinson take a kickoff, reverse his field three times, and return the ball all the way for a touchdown. He became my boyhood idol.

Little did I realize at the time that only a few years later I would take Pete Reiser's place in center field for the Dodgers, that Reese would become my teammate and one of my closest friends, and that I would be witness to history when Jackie Robinson became the first black man to play major league baseball.

By the time I reached high school I had become a pretty good baseball player, and the scouts started coming around. I also played basketball and football and made all-star teams in all three sports, but baseball was my first love. Dad occasionally took me to Wrigley Field to watch the Los Angeles Angels, the Cubs' farm team in the Pacific Coast League. That was before the major leagues went west.

In old Wrigley Field I embraced my first baseball hero, the Angels' little center fielder and leadoff hitter named Jigger Statz, a former major leaguer who had played with the Giants, Red Sox, Cubs, and Dodgers. I suppose I was attracted by his unusual name.

I graduated from Compton High School in February 1944, and I was faced with having to choose my future. I had offers to go to college to play football, basketball, or baseball. There were other options: join the military; get a job; sign a professional baseball contract. I opted for the latter.

At the time, my dad was in the navy serving in the South Pacific. He was in the navy as a young man, before I was born, and when World War II broke out, he rejoined because he loved the navy life and because he figured that if he was already in the service, I wouldn't be taken when I was of draft age. I had no older brothers or sisters, so it was just my mom and me left to make the decision about my future.

I told Mom that I wanted to play baseball, and she accepted my decision. Then I had to decide which one of three offers to accept, the one from the Pittsburgh Pirates, the Cincinnati Reds, or the Brooklyn Dodgers. I could have received more money from the Pirates or Reds, but because the Dodgers were my favorite team, I accepted their offer: a bonus of $750, a salary of $250 per month, and $1.25 per day in meal money—you could eat for $1.25 a day in 1944.

I have never regretted my decision to sign with the Dodgers, not for a minute. I was so blessed to be on that team in the fifties. It was a perfect fit for me, being the only left-handed hitter and playing in such a good hitter's ballpark as Ebbets Field. I got to play alongside great players like Jackie Robinson, Pete Reiser, and Andy Pafko, three of my earliest heroes, and to form lifelong friendships with Pee Wee Reese, Gil Hodges, Carl Erskine, Rube Walker, Don Zimmer, Roy Campanella, and Johnny Podres. And I got to play in New York City during the golden age of baseball, when the city was home to three major league teams—three great teams—the Dodgers, Giants, and Yankees.

There was a lot of talk back then, debates about who was better. Roy Campanella or Yogi Berra? Phil Rizzuto or Pee Wee Reese? Mickey Mantle, Willie Mays, or Duke Snider? That was all media talk and fan talk. There were Yankees and Giants fans in Brooklyn, Giants and Dodgers fans in the Bronx, Yankees and Dodgers fans in Manhattan, and those arguments would rage throughout the summer on street corners and in bars.

The players never got involved in those discussions. As far as we were concerned, there was no personal rivalry. Speaking personally, I was flattered to be included in comparisons with the two all-time great players Mantle and Mays, and also flattered that the comparison has been perpetuated by Terry Cashman's popular song, "Talkin' Baseball—Willie, Mickey, and the Duke."

But there was no rivalry. The media made it a rivalry. The fans made it a rivalry. I never cared what Mantle and Mays did as long as we won. I didn't pick up the newspaper and look at the box scores to see what they were hitting. I didn't care. I was just hoping they lost—the Giants, anyway. I couldn't care less if the Yankees won or lost.

I got to be pretty good friends with Mantle and Mays, especially after we all retired. Mickey and I got along really well. I used to see him at banquets, golf tournaments, and card shows, and I always enjoyed being around him. I looked forward to our meetings, and I think he did too. Mickey always seemed more comfortable around ballplayers than he did around other people.

Willie and I were teammates for one year, my final season, 1964, when the Mets sold me to the Giants. One day I was in the lineup playing left field in Candlestick Park. I was the left fielder and Willie was the center fielder. The national anthem was playing and I was standing about a foot off the left-field line when I yelled over to Mays, "Hey, Willie. All these years I've been reading how great you are. This is mine, you've got everything else."

Willie just looked at me and said, "You're crazy, man!"

At the card shows I also would run into two of the greatest players the game has known, Joe DiMaggio and Ted Williams. I had seen both of them play in the Pacific Coast League when I was a kid. If I was at a card show and DiMaggio was there, I would sneak up behind him and say, "There's my favorite center fielder." He'd know it was me, and we'd spend some time together talking baseball.

Williams was another guy I enjoyed seeing at card shows because he loved to talk baseball and was so interesting and analytical, especially on the subject of hitting. One day, long after we had both retired, we were at a card show together and Ted called over to me and, in that loud bellowing voice of his, said, "Hey, Duke, how many home runs did you hit?"

"Four hundred and seven," I replied.

A few seconds passed. "Well," he boomed, "you're not going to hit any more."

I cherish the time I spent in Brooklyn. New York in the fifties was a special time in baseball. Those were great days, and the Yankees, Giants, and Dodgers were great teams.

To me, the greatest team I ever played on was the 1952 Brooklyn Dodgers. The Giants had beaten us for of the National League pennant in 1951 on Bobby Thomson's ninth-inning home run in the third playoff game, but we got our revenge in 1952 by winning the pennant, four and a half games ahead of the Giants, and met the Yankees in the World Series.

We went ahead in the Series, three games to two, when Carl Erskine pitched 11 innings in Game 5, retired the last 19 Yankees, and beat them, 6–5. I doubled home Billy Cox in the eleventh for what proved to be the winning run, and we returned to Brooklyn needing to win one of the next two games to bring Brooklyn its first World Series championship.

In Game 6, I hit two home runs off Vic Raschi. Unfortunately, both came with nobody on base. The Yankees got solo homers from Mantle and Berra and scored a third run when Raschi got a single on a ball that hit our pitcher, Billy Loes, on the knee. (Loes later said he lost the ground ball in the sun.) We got beat, 3–2, and it all came down to Game 7.

That was the game in which Casey Stengel used all three of his top starters, Eddie Lopat, Allie Reynolds, and Raschi. We had loaded the bases with one out in the bottom of the seventh and the Yankees ahead 4–2, when Stengel went to the mound to remove Raschi and bring in left-hander Bob Kuzava to face me.

The move didn't faze me. I always hit Kuzava well when I faced him in the minor leagues. As Kuzava was taking his warm-up pitches, I walked over to

Jackie Robinson in the on-deck circle and said, "Well, Jack, we've been wait-ing for this for a long time, and it's up to you and me. I'd just as soon get it over with."

"Yeah," Jackie said. "I'd like to see you get it over with too. Whack one and get us two or three runs."

I worked the count to 3–2, fouled off a few pitches, and then popped one on the left side of the infield for the second out. I was disappointed, but I returned to the bench confident Jackie would get a hit and drive in the tying runs.

Once again the count went to 3–2, which meant that the runners would be off with the next pitch, a big advantage for us. A single would score two runs; a double could mean three and the lead. Kuzava jammed Jackie with a fastball, and Jackie popped it up on the infield near first base. Kuzava looked at first baseman Joe Collins. Collins looked at Kuzava. Neither of them moved. Collins apparently had lost the ball in the sun, and it was falling rap-idly as three Dodgers raced madly around the bases. If the ball hit the ground two runs, maybe three, would score. Out of nowhere came Billy Martin, the second baseman. He made a mad dash and caught the ball at his shoe tops, inches from the ground.

I had no idea how Martin caught that ball. I still don't know. But he did, and with it went our last chance to win the game. Kuzava held us hitless over the last two innings, and we were beaten again.

That was one time the better team did not win. I thought then, and I still think, that the 1952 Dodgers were a better team than the Yankees, and the best team I ever played on.

Or maybe it was the 1953 team, which won 105 games and finished 13 games ahead of the Milwaukee Braves. How many teams can you think of that had four future Hall of Famers—Robinson, Reese, Campanella, and me—in their starting lineup? It also had a batting champion, Furillo; an RBI champion, Campy; a 20-game winner, Erskine; five .300 hitters, Hodges, Furillo, Robinson, Campanella, and myself; and five players with more than 90 RBIs, Campy, Hodges, me, Furillo, and Robinson.

Again, we lost the World Series to the Yankees, this time in six games.

As a result, in picking my all-time Dodgers team I included a lot of the members of those 1952 and 1953 teams on my lists. I admit to a certain bias when it comes to the 1952 and 1953 Dodgers, but if you check the record books, you'll agree that I have no reason to apologize for picking any of them.

Selecting an all-time team for any franchise is never easy and is always going to stir some controversy, especially when there are so many great players that came before me that I never saw play. But history will confirm that the greatest decades in Dodgers history were the fifties, sixties, and seventies, and so my all-time Dodgers team is well stocked with players from those three decades.

—Duke Snider

ONE

Catcher

Roy Campanella's place in baseball history is secure as one of only 14 catchers in the Hall of Fame. Where Campy rates among those 14 is open to debate, but imagine if the start of his major league career had not been delayed by a shameful unwritten code that excluded blacks, or if his career had not been short circuited by the tragic automobile accident that left him a quadriplegic.

He might have been regarded as the number one catcher in baseball history.

Campy was already 26 years old and had been a star in the Negro Leagues when he joined the Dodgers in 1948. And he was only 36 years old when he had his accident in 1958. He certainly could have played another two or three seasons, and he certainly would have added to his 242 career home runs and 856 RBIs, given the Los Angeles Coliseum's short fence in left field, 250 feet away, and in left center, 320 feet away.

1. ROY CAMPANELLA

2. JOHN ROSEBORO

3. STEVE YEAGER

4. MIKE PIAZZA

5. AL LOPEZ

Campanella was born in Philadelphia. Although he was half Italian on his father's side, his mother was black, and that was enough to prevent him from playing in the major leagues prior to 1947.

*I*t was 1951, a year that will live in infamy in Brooklyn and be renowned across the Harlem River in Manhattan. The Giants, 13½ games behind the Dodgers on August 11, put on a furious rush, while the Dodgers played mediocre baseball and watched their once seemingly insurmountable lead melt away like ice cream in the hot summer sun.

As the days dwindled down to a precious few, Monte Irvin of the Giants and Roy Campanella of the Dodgers—friends, former stars of the Negro Leagues, and field leaders of their respective teams—engaged in a mano a mano duel attempting to carry their teams to the finish line on their backs. They were contemporaries in the Negro Leagues, teammates in the Puerto Rico Winter League in 1941, and entered the National League at about the same time, Campanella in 1948, Irvin the following year. Two years after that, they were key figures in the most famous race between baseball's most intense rivals, the Dodgers versus the Giants (think of the Yankees versus the Red Sox and double it).

In the end it came down to the second three-game playoff in National League history, and the Giants prevailed on the most memorable home run in the history of the game, a walk-off, three-run blast by Bobby Thomson in the bottom of the ninth inning of the third game. Campanella, with a batting average of .325, 33 home runs, and 108 RBIs, won the first of his three Most Valuable Player awards. But it was little consolation to the competitive Campy. He would have gladly traded the hardware for another World Series. Irvin, who batted .312, hit 24 home runs, and led the league with 121 RBIs, finished third in the MVP voting. If there was disappointment, it never surfaced. His team had won the pennant, and that was reward enough for Irvin.

"They were our arch enemies," Irvin said of the Dodgers. "There was a lot of bad blood between us, and a lot of their guys we didn't like. But not Campanella. He was my favorite. There was nobody who didn't like Campy and Pee Wee Reese. I had the highest regard for Campanella as a man and as a player. He was smart, he was feisty, he was a great competitor, and he was very talented. And he was a good guy."

How good a catcher?

Irvin answers that question:

A great catcher. But I couldn't say he was the greatest. There have been a lot of great catchers, like [Bill] Dickey, [Mickey] Cochrane, [Gabby] Hartnett, [Yogi] Berra, and [Johnny] Bench. I can't say Campy was better than any of them, but he's right up there with all of them.

The greatest? I played against Josh Gibson in the Negro Leagues and with him in All-Star Games, and I never saw anybody like him. Campy was a little better catcher than Gibson, but as a hitter, Gibson was the best I've seen. He's in a class by himself. You can't compare anybody to Josh Gibson. Not Campanella, not Willie Mays, not Ted Williams, not Joe DiMaggio, not Hank Aaron, not even Babe Ruth. Nobody.

When he was 15 years old, Campy started playing for a semipro team, the Bacharach Giants. He was so impressive that the Baltimore Elite Giants of the Negro National League offered him a contract. Because of his age, Campy could play only on weekends. The following year, he quit school and joined the team full-time.

By 1939 he was a star and was challenging the great Josh Gibson, who was getting old, as the top catcher in the Negro Leagues. Campy told me a lot about Gibson. He said Gibson was the greatest hitter he'd ever seen. Campy was not too shabby himself. He would play in the Negro National League for nine years, many of which he could have spent adding to his major league numbers had he been given the chance.

That chance finally came in 1946 when Branch Rickey signed five black players, including Robinson and Campanella. Roy was ready for the major leagues then, but the major leagues weren't ready for him, so he spent 1946 with the Dodgers' Class B team in Nashua, New Hampshire, where he roomed with Don Newcombe and was managed by Walter Alston, and then spent 1947 with their top farm team in Montreal.

Campy came to the Dodgers in 1948, played in 83 games, hit nine home runs, drove in 45 runs, and batted .258. His arrival enabled the Dodgers to move Gil Hodges, who had been a catcher, to first base, a move that would strengthen the Dodgers in two positions and help them to win five pennants in the next eight years.

Along the way Campanella would lead the league in RBIs with 142; set a single-season major league record for home runs by a catcher with 41 in 1953; hit over .300 three times; and win three National League Most Valuable Player awards, in 1951, 1953, and 1955.

I had all the respect in the world for Campanella. He was one of the guys, a delightful man, and a lot of fun to be around—and a great, great catcher. His personality was much different from Robinson's. Where Jackie was militant and played the game with a chip on his shoulder, Campy was

Roy Campanella successfully tags out Giants base runner Daryl Spencer after taking the throw from right fielder Carl Furillo in a 1953 game at Ebbets Field.

a happy man—fun loving and outgoing with a great sense of humor. His pleasant disposition and his enthusiasm were infectious.

Campy was a jovial, roly-poly guy who used to arrive in the clubhouse wearing a Panama hat and with a big cigar in his mouth. If we had won the day before, he'd walk in and shout, "Same team that won yesterday is gonna win today."

As a catcher, Roy was durable. One day we were in Philadelphia. It was hot and humid, and we had a doubleheader scheduled, so I asked Roy if he could catch both games.

"Hell," he said, "I caught four games in one day in the Negro Leagues, so why can't I catch two in the big leagues?"

Campy had a great arm, and he was very intelligent about the game. I imagine that at the time it was hard for a black man to handle a pitching staff that was all white, but Campy earned their respect and their confidence because of his ability and his knowledge.

When he was at Nashua, New Hampshire, Alston had so much respect for Campy that one day, when Alston was ejected from a game, he turned the lineup card over to Roy and had him manage the game, even though Campanella was just a rookie.

Some people have suggested that Campanella, not Robinson, should have been the one to break the color barrier. I don't agree. Campy's easygoing, happy-go-lucky disposition would not have been right for the situation. Jackie was the right choice, as history has proved.

However, I believe Campy would have made a good major league manager, but that Robinson wouldn't have. Jackie was better suited to be a general manager.

It's no accident that so many former catchers became outstanding managers, all the way back to Connie Mack and Wilbert Robinson; to Al Lopez, Birdie Tebbetts, Ralph Houk, and Gil Hodges; right up to today with Joe Torre, Mike Scioscia, and Bruce Bochy.

Without a doubt, given the chance, Campanella would have been a great manager, the first successful black manager. He probably would not have been one for the Dodgers because Alston was there for 23 years, but some other team would have given him the chance to be a manager, and he would have been a good one.

When he was at Nashua, New Hampshire, Alston had so much respect for Campy that one day, when Alston was ejected from a game, he turned the

5

lineup card over to Roy and had him manage the game, even though Campanella was just a rookie. Let it be recorded for history that Roy Campanella was the first black man to manage a game in organized baseball, even if it was for just one game. And, by the way, Nashua won the game, so Campy's record as a manager is 1–0, and his winning percentage as a manager is a perfect 1.000.

Some people might question whether Campy, with his easy, outgoing nature, would have been tough enough as a manager. I don't think he would have had a problem. I can't imagine that any players would have taken advantage of him because they would have had a great deal of respect for him, as I did.

Put yourself in **John Roseboro**'s place. He came to the Brooklyn Dodgers in 1957 as a 24-year-old kid, and Roy Campanella was the catcher, so Roseboro didn't get to play very much. He caught a few games, played a little first base.

The next year the Dodgers moved to L.A. and, during the winter, Campy had that awful automobile accident that left him paralyzed. They gave the catching job to Rube Walker, who had been Campy's backup for years, but the Los Angeles Coliseum just ate up Rube, as it did so many left-handed hitters.

The Coliseum was built for football, but it became the Dodgers' temporary home until Dodger Stadium was built. Because of the way the Coliseum was constructed—430 to 440 feet to right center—it was deadly for us left-handed hitters. Rube would hit 400-foot outs, and we used to kid him that the Coliseum made him a manager in Atlanta.

With Walker struggling, Roseboro moved in to take over the catching duties. He became the Dodgers' number one catcher, taking the place of the great Campy. Talk about being under pressure!

But it was never really discussed around the ballclub. Campy wasn't around Los Angeles much in those days; he was still back East undergoing physical therapy. He didn't start coming around until a few years later.

I'm sure the fact that he was trying to replace a future Hall of Famer entered Roseboro's mind. It certainly was written about, but Gabby—Roseboro's nickname, which in baseball parlance means he didn't say much, but when he said something, one paid attention—handled the situation, and the pressure, beautifully. He was that kind of guy. He took over for Campy and became an outstanding catcher. He handled that great Dodgers pitching staff of Koufax, Drysdale, and Podres.

Roseboro was a very fierce competitor, and he was tough, a former football player. The way he made the tag play at home plate, you could see he liked contact. He dumped quite a few guys. He was as good as any catcher I ever saw at blocking home plate.

Catcher John Roseboro rushes out to greet Sandy Koufax after Koufax stopped the Yankees, 2–1, to complete a sweep of the 1963 World Series.

John made himself into an outstanding catcher. He was great at handling pitchers, and he threw very well. Very accurately. And very intelligently. He knew how to play baseball. In 1959, when we won the World Series in L.A., Roseboro was one of the big reasons for the win.

Just recently I was talking with Johnny Podres about Roseboro. Johnny said, "Roseboro was an interesting guy. I sat down with him one day and was talking with him, and he said, 'You know, Johnny, I'm catching some awful good pitchers. Koufax is the best. He's easy to catch except when he throws that overhand curve that starts head high and breaks down into the dirt. Drysdale is probably the most erratic of all the pitchers to catch because of the movement on his ball. You were the easiest to catch, Johnny, but the toughest to work with. You shook me off all the time.'"

He might not have intended to hit Marichal, but I have no doubt that the old football player mentality in John came out and he purposely threw the ball past Marichal's ear to intimidate him.

A lot of people hear the name John Roseboro and think of the brawl he had with Juan Marichal in 1965, and that's unfortunate.

Marichal was at bat, and when Roseboro threw the ball back to the pitcher, it whistled past Marichal's ear. The next thing we knew, Marichal was hitting Roseboro on top of the head with his bat, and then all hell broke loose.

Juan later claimed that the ball had nicked his ear and implied that Roseboro did it on purpose. Knowing John Roseboro as I do, I can say that he probably did do it deliberately. He might not have intended to hit Marichal, but I have no doubt that the old football player mentality in John came out and he purposely threw the ball past Marichal's ear to intimidate him. That was John Roseboro, the ultimate competitor. Anything to win a game.

Steve Yeager was the first catcher to wear the neck protector, the leather flap that hangs down from the catcher's mask and covers his throat. It all came about, as many inventions do, as the result of a near-tragic accident.

Ironically, Yeager wasn't catching at the time of his accident; he was in the on-deck circle. The Dodgers were playing in San Diego, and Bill Russell was batting. He swung at an inside pitch and broke his bat, just splintered it. A piece of the barrel went flying toward the Dodgers dugout. Somebody yelled, "Look out," and Yeager looked up to have the jagged end of the bat pierce his throat. It just stuck in his throat and stayed there.

8

Bill Buhler, the Dodgers trainer, went running out, and so did the San Diego trainer. I wasn't there to see it, but people who were said it was a frightening sight. Luckily, Buhler used his head and his training and reacted quickly. He probably saved Yeager's life. Bill held the bat in Yeager's throat because he was afraid it had hit an artery or a vein—if it had and they removed the bat, Yeager would have bled to death. By keeping the bat in Yeager's throat, they helped to stem the bleeding.

It must have been a strange sight when the ambulance came and they carried Yeager off the field on a stretcher, still holding the bat in his throat. It wasn't until they got him to the hospital that they removed the bat.

Steve Yeager jumps over a sliding Bob Watson after forcing Watson at the plate on a squeeze play during the 1981 World Series.

Fortunately, no artery or vein was ruptured, so they stitched Yeager up and he was back playing within a week. To protect the wound, Buhler devised the attachment that hangs down from the mask and covers the throat. Catchers still use the mask with the throat attachment today.

I've heard a lot of pitchers rave about how great it was to pitch to Yeager, who played on seven division winners. He called a great game. He was tough. He was a team leader. And he was practically flawless defensively. Lou Brock said he was the best-throwing catcher in the game.

Yeager wasn't a great hitter—he had only a .228 lifetime average—but he had some pop in his bat and he got a lot of big hits for the Dodgers, including a game-winning home run off Ron Guidry in Game 5 of the 1981 World Series.

I rate **Mike Piazza** only fourth among Dodgers catchers because he was a Dodger for only a little more than five years and because of his defensive deficiencies, which have been well documented.

His defensive liabilities are all hearsay to me, though. You'd hear that he didn't call a good game and he didn't work well with pitchers, but that was early in his career and he was still learning. No question Mike's true value has been in his bat. It is awesome to watch him hit. Not only is he the all-time leader in home runs for a catcher, but he has been a consistent .300 hitter with a career batting average well over .300. His .362 average in 1997 is the highest ever for a Dodgers catcher and the seventh highest by a Dodger at any position. Not bad for a guy who doesn't run well enough to get any leg hits.

Mike will finish his career with a lifetime batting average around .315, which is better than 12 of the 14 catchers currently in the Hall of Fame (only Mickey Cochrane's, at .320, is higher). Piazza's career average is some 45 points higher than Johnny Bench's, Carlton Fisk's, and Gary Carter's; 40 points higher than Roy Campanella's; and 30 points higher than Yogi Berra's.

One can make the case that Mike Piazza is the greatest-hitting catcher in baseball history.

The remarkable thing about Piazza is that he wasn't even considered a prospect when he was drafted. The Dodgers took him in the 62nd round and only as a favor to manager Tommy Lasorda, who was a buddy of Piazza's father's back in Pennsylvania.

Mike Piazza fires to first base to complete a double play after forcing San Diego's Scott Livingstone at the plate during a game in 1996.

When I first saw Piazza, I thought he was Hall of Fame material. One night I took my two grandsons to Dodger Stadium, and we watched the Dodgers take batting practice. Piazza stepped into the batting cage, and we were standing behind it watching him. Piazza hit one into the left-field pavilion, and my little grandson Jordan said to his brother, "Brandon, did you see how far that one went?" Mike was just smoking them.

In his five-plus seasons with the Dodgers, Piazza hit 177 home runs, drove in 563 runs, and batted .331, which is fourth on the Dodgers all-time list and

Al Lopez was regarded as one of the best defensive catchers of all time, and then he went on to become a Hall of Fame manager.

is by far the highest lifetime average of any Dodger after the team moved to Los Angeles. He undoubtedly would have ended up in the top 10, or better, in every major offensive department on the Dodgers all-time list, but he was traded to Florida in 1998, which was a business decision. The Dodgers probably didn't want to pay him the millions they knew he would command. Unfortunately, they have never been able to replace his bat.

I never saw **Al Lopez** play, but I knew him. He was the manager of the Chicago White Sox when we played them in the 1959 World Series. A wonderful man. A good man. Everything I ever heard about him indicated that he was a top-notch catcher. He knew the game, and he handled his pitchers very well.

He wasn't much of a hitter. He had a career batting average of .261 and in 19 seasons never hit more than eight home runs or drove in more than 57 runs, but he was regarded as one of the greatest defensive catchers ever. And he was durable. When he retired, he had caught 1,918 games, the most in baseball history at the time.

Lopez made his mark, and was elected to the Hall of Fame, as a manager, another of the many former catchers who became outstanding managers. His combined record as a manager with the Cleveland Indians and Chicago White Sox was 1,410–1,004. That's a winning percentage of .584, which was ninth all-time when he retired.

His misfortune was coming up against the great Yankees teams. From 1951 to 1964, the Yankees won the American League pennant 12 times. The only times they did not win the AL pennant, they were beaten by teams managed by Lopez—Cleveland in 1954 and Chicago in 1959. In every other year of the fifties, Lopez's teams finished second to the Yanks.

In 1954 Lopez's Indians won a then–league record 111 games and then were beaten in the World Series by the Giants in a four-game sweep. This man, who was called "El Señor," passed away in 2005 at the age of 97. He had a long, wonderful, and productive life and was still very sharp mentally at that advanced age.

Until his death, he was the oldest living member of the Hall of Fame and the last White Sox manager to win a pennant—the 1959 team that lost to us in the World Series—until the Sox won in 2005.

I hope it was some consolation to Lopez that he lived long enough to see his beloved White Sox win their first World Series in 88 years.

13

Statistical Summaries

All statistics are for player's Dodgers career only.

HITTING

G = Games
H = Hits
HR = Home runs
RBI = Runs batted in
SB = Stolen bases
BA = Batting average

Catcher	Years	G	H	HR	RBI	SB	BA
Roy Campanella *Caught three no-hitters (Erskine in 1952 and 1956, Maglie in 1956)*	1948–57	1,215	1,161	242	856	25	.276
John Roseboro *Led league in total chances per game five straight years from 1958 to 1962*	1957–67	1,289	1,009	92	471	59	.251
Steve Yeager *Homered twice in both 1977 and 1981 World Series*	1972–85	1,219	789	100	398	14	.228

continued	Years	G	H	HR	RBI	SB	BA
Mike Piazza *Second in MVP voting in both 1996 and 1997*	1992–98	726	896	177	563	10	.331
Al Lopez *Led league in assists and fielding average three times*	1928 1930–35	762	665	20	274	21	.274

FIELDING

PO = Putouts

A = Assists

E = Errors

DP = Double plays

TC/G — Total chances divided by games played

FA = Fielding average

Catcher	PO	A	E	DP	TC/G	FA
Roy Campanella	6,520	550	85	82	6.0	.988
John Roseboro	7,895	565	87	89	7.0	.990
Steve Yeager	5,876	652	88	70	5.6	.987
Mike Piazza	4,815	365	58	43	7.5	.989
Al Lopez	2,783	428	60	51	4.4	.982

TWO

First Baseman

So beloved was **Gil Hodges** in Brooklyn that instead of booing him when he was in a slump, people prayed for him. The strong, silent type, and a former Marine, Hodges exuded power, grace, and goodness.

More than any other Dodger, Brooklyn fans embraced Gil as one of their own—and he was. Born in Indiana, he married a Brooklyn girl, and they made their home in Brooklyn. When the Dodgers left for Los Angeles, Hodges went with them but returned to Brooklyn in the off-season and then came back to play for the New York Mets.

After two years with the Mets, Gil left again to manage the Washington Senators and then came back once more to manage the Miracle Mets, the team that shocked the baseball world by beating the Baltimore Orioles in the 1969 World Series.

1. GIL HODGES

2. DOLPH CAMILLI

3. STEVE GARVEY

4. WES PARKER

5. EDDIE MURRAY

I don't remember ever thinking of Gil as a potential manager when we were players. He knew the game, all right, but it just never occurred to me he had ambitions to manage. When he got the chance with the Mets, he

Gil Hodges was one of the most beloved Dodgers of all time, and after his playing career he went on to manage the Miracle Mets of 1969.

became an excellent manager and a strong leader who had the respect of his players. More than respect—there might even have been a little fear.

Gil was such an imposing physical specimen that when he said something, you listened . . . and you obeyed because you didn't want to find out what the consequences would be if you didn't.

Gil and I came up to the Dodgers at the same time, in 1947. He became my roommate and my friend forever. Although he was soft-spoken and had a reputation of being a gentle giant, Gil had a sense of humor and a little devil in him too. He liked to play practical jokes.

That first year Gil and I shared a room in a private home on Bedford Avenue, not far from Ebbets Field. Hodges was the third-string catcher (in

1943 at the age of 19 he actually played one game for the Dodgers at third base before going off to the Marines), and I was the sixth outfielder.

One day Branch Rickey called us into his office and said, "In a few years, you two guys are going to be the leading power hitters on this ballclub."

Gil and I looked at each other without saying anything, and Rickey kept telling us how good we were going to be. Then we got up and left, and I said to Gil, "If we're going to be that good, how come we're not playing now?"

Gil said, "I guess we have a lot to learn."

Two years later we were both starting and Rickey's prediction had come true. For the next nine seasons Gil and I both hit at least 20 home runs. Gil extended his streak two more years, giving him 11 straight years with at least 20 home runs, and he also drove in more than 100 runs for seven straight seasons.

There was one especially magical night for Gil against the Boston Braves in Brooklyn in 1950. It was August 31, and Gil became only the sixth player in baseball history to hit four home runs in a game, and only the third (the others were Lou Gehrig and Chuck Klein) to do it in a nine-inning game in the modern era (after 1903). Gil also hit a single and drove in nine runs in the 19–3 romp over the Braves.

Hodges was a good catcher, and he would have been a great one, but when Roy Campanella came along, the Dodgers moved Gil to first base, which turned out to be a pretty good move.

Leo Durocher once said, "With my catching set, I put a first baseman's glove on our other rookie catcher, Gil Hodges, and told him to have some fun. Three days later I looked up and, wow, I was looking at the best first baseman I'd seen since Dolph Camilli."

Hodges had large hands, so big that we used to kid him that he didn't even need a glove. And he had good hands, soft hands. If he failed to come up with a throw, I'd say to myself, "Gil must not be feeling very well today," because normally those balls wouldn't get by him. It was surprising to me when a ball did get by him. He was like a vacuum cleaner. He sucked everything up.

There have been a lot of good-fielding first basemen, but Hodges was the best I ever saw. And what made that so unusual is that most of the great first basemen are left-handed throwers, and Gil threw right-handed. First base has traditionally been a left-handed thrower's position. A lefty has an easier time making the difficult, but important, first-to-shortstop-to-first double play.

Gil made that play better than any right-handed thrower, and most left-handed throwers, I've ever seen. He also was great on bunts. If there were runners on first and second and the hitter put down a bunt, Gil would charge the ball and throw the runner out at third. And being a right-handed thrower made it an even tougher play.

The 1952 World Series against the Yankees was a nightmare for Hodges. He was hitless for the entire Series, 0 for 21. His slump continued into the next season, and that's when they prayed for Gil. Gil went to mass at his church, St. Francis Xavier, one Sunday, and the pastor got up in the pulpit and said, "It's too hot for a sermon, so I suggest that you go home, keep the commandments, and say a prayer for Gil Hodges."

Those prayers were answered. Gil finished the season batting .302 with 31 home runs and 122 RBIs, and he batted .364 in the 1953 World Series.

In almost 60 years in baseball, I've seen many great first basemen, like Vic Power, Andres Galarraga, Wes Parker, Keith Hernandez, and Don Mattingly, but Gil Hodges is in a class by himself, and that's why I can't understand why Gil is not in the Hall of Fame.

The day before Opening Day in 1947, my first year with the Dodgers, John Griffin, the longtime clubhouse man for the Dodgers—they called him "the Senator"—came up to me and said, "What number do you want?"

I had been wearing a number in the 20s during spring training and now the Senator was giving me my choice of numbers, which meant I had made the ballclub. I asked him, "What's available?"

Pee Wee Reese had No. 1, and Leo Durocher, who was suspended that year, had worn No. 2, so they were saving that number for when he came back. But No. 3 and No. 4 were available, so I said, "How about No. 4?"

Lou Gehrig had worn No. 4 for the Yankees, and Mel Ott wore that number with the Giants, a couple of pretty good left-handed power hitters, Hall of Famers. It seemed like a good fit.

"That was **Dolph Camilli**'s number," Griffin said. "You're a left-handed power hitter. Why not?"

And that's how I came to be No. 4.

At the time, I knew a little about Camilli. He was the cleanup hitter on the Dodgers of my youth, the 1941 National League championship team. Later, I heard a lot about him from Reese. Pee Wee told me how good Dolph

Dolph Camilli reaches for a high throw during his first spring workout as a Dodger, in 1938 in Clearwater, Florida.

was. He said Camilli was an outstanding first baseman, the best the Dodgers had until Gil Hodges came along.

I met Camilli after the Dodgers moved to Los Angeles. His son, Doug, was a catcher who came up through the Dodgers' farm system and was my teammate for a few seasons, and Dolph would come to the ballpark to see Doug. I was struck by the fact that Dolph had so much power for such a little guy—only 5'10" and about 185 pounds—but he was strong. He had done some boxing early in his life. In fact, in the movie *Cinderella Man*, which is about heavyweight champion James J. Braddock, the climax is when Braddock takes the title from Max Baer. In the movie Baer is portrayed as a killer in the ring because two men died after they fought him. One of those two, a heavyweight named Frankie Campbell, was Dolph Camilli's brother.

Camilli's contribution to the Dodgers' success was not just on the field. He provided veteran leadership and a calm, low-key demeanor that was a perfect antidote to manager Leo Durocher's fiery, excitable, and irascible personality.

Camilli came out of San Francisco and got to the big leagues with the Chicago Cubs in 1933. The following year he was traded to Philadelphia, where he became a star. From 1935 to 1937 he hit 80 home runs for the Phillies. When Larry MacPhail left Cincinnati and took over as president of the Dodgers in 1938, the first player he went after was Camilli. MacPhail was able to get him for a journeyman outfielder named Eddie Morgan and $45,000, which, I'm sure, was the main reason the Phillies were willing to part with Camilli.

In Brooklyn Camilli was a major reason the Dodgers became a contender and, eventually, won the pennant in 1941, their first pennant in 21 years. In his first three years in Brooklyn, Dolph hit 73 home runs and drove in exactly 300 runs. Then came his breakout 1941 season. Camilli led the National League in home runs with 34 and RBIs with 120 and was named the league's Most Valuable Player.

Camilli's contribution to the Dodgers' success was not just on the field. He provided veteran leadership and a calm, low-key demeanor that was a perfect antidote to manager Leo Durocher's fiery, excitable, and irascible personality.

Camilli followed up his MVP year with another big season in 1942, hitting 26 homers and driving in 109 runs, but in 1943 it was obvious he was coming to the end of the line. By July 31, he had just six home runs and 43 RBIs and was traded to the Giants. But Camilli had too much pride and so refused to report to the hated Giants.

I knew **Steve Garvey** before I knew him, and if that sounds like a Yogi Berraism, let me explain. Garvey's dad was the driver of our bus during spring training in Vero Beach, Florida. At the time Steve would have been a little guy, about six or seven years old, and I probably saw him around, but I can't honestly say I remember.

There are a lot of similarities between Garvey and Gil Hodges. Both were the strong, silent type and right-handed power hitters. Like Hodges, Garvey came up as a third baseman (Gil played his first major league game at third base), was moved to first base, and made himself into a good first baseman by hard work—good enough to win four Gold Gloves. He was excellent at coming up with low throws. He handled himself very well at first base, but he was no Gil Hodges (there was only one Gil), and I don't say that to disparage Garvey because I have a lot of respect for him. He got the job done.

Offensively, Garvey was a great clutch-hitter and the Dodgers' leader—their first baseman and big run producer for 10 years, during which they won four pennants and one World Series. In that 10-year period, Garvey hit more than 20 home runs five times, drove in more than 100 runs five times, and batted over .300 seven times. His big year was 1974, when he batted .312, hit 21 homers, drove in 111 runs, and was named Most Valuable Player in the National League. That year he made the All-Star team as a write-in candidate and wound up being named MVP of the game.

Garvey also was one of the most durable players of his time. He played in a National League–record 1,207 consecutive games from 1975 to 1983. He was such a favorite in Los Angeles that a junior high school was named after him while he was still an active player.

Dodgers fans were devastated when, after the 1982 season, Garvey left the Dodgers to sign a lucrative free-agent contract with the San Diego Padres, just down the road from L.A. It was typical of Garvey that on his first trip with the Padres to Los Angeles, he took out a full-page ad in an L.A. newspaper thanking Dodgers fans for their past support.

Although he helped the Padres get to their first World Series in 1984, Garvey wasn't the same player in San Diego that he had been with the Dodgers, largely because the one-time iron man of the Dodgers battled a series of injuries. But when he retired after the 1987 season, Garvey had accumulated a .294 average, 272 home runs, and 1,308 RBIs in 19 seasons, which are pretty close to Hall of Fame numbers if you ask me.

As far back as he can remember, Steve Garvey wanted to be a Dodger. Growing up in Vero Beach, Florida, the young Garvey spent much of his spare time in the spring at the Dodgers' spring-training base. His father drove the Dodgers' bus and took young Steve along on many of the trips.

Garvey's boyhood dream came true in 1969, when he was a late-season call-up for the Dodgers and appeared in three games as a pinch-hitter. Over the next two seasons, he would appear in 115 games, 106 of them at third base. By 1972 the Dodgers had decided Garvey was their third baseman of the future, a decision based on their desire to get his booming bat into the lineup on a regular basis.

In the winter between the 1971 and 1972 seasons, the Dodgers began revamping their team by trading slugger Dick Allen to the Chicago White Sox for veteran left-hander Tommy John, already the possessor of 84 major league victories. John's stock-in-trade was a sinkerball, and his success was predicated on his having excellent infield defense behind him. As such, Tommy was in for a bit of a shock when he arrived in Los Angeles.

"When I got to the Dodgers in 1972," said John, "their infield was Wes Parker at first, Jim Lefebvre at second, Maury Wills at short, and Steve Garvey at third. Garvey was horrible at third base. He could field the ball, field shots, but he couldn't throw it across the infield. If it hadn't been for Parker, Garve would have had 100 errors."

In fact, Garvey made 28 errors in 85 games at third base, an inordinate number, and John may have paid the price. He won only 11 games. The Dodgers knew they had overestimated Garvey's ability to handle third base.

"Toward the end of the season," said John, "they gave Garve a first baseman's glove. Parker had announced his retirement and everybody thought Bill Buckner or Tom Paciorek was going to get the first base job, but they gave Garvey a first baseman's glove and said, 'Take it over because we have a kid down in Triple A ball who can play third.' The Penguin. Ron Cey."

For several years this switch of positions reaped benefits for Garvey, John, and the Dodgers.

Steve Garvey, who grew up longing to become a Dodger, wins a game with a bases-loaded single against the Phillies in 1981.

> "Garve made himself into a pretty good first baseman," said John.
>
> In his first season at the new position, Garvey made only five errors in 76 games. Released from the burden of playing third base, Garvey's hitting also improved. He batted .304 with eight homers and 50 RBIs. Not coincidentally, with better infield defense behind him, John won 16 games.
>
> Over the next five seasons, John won 60 games for the Dodgers (although he missed all of 1975 for ligament-replacement surgery). Garvey batted .297 or better all five years, drove in 95 or more runs four times, hit 20 or more home runs three times, and was the National League's Most Valuable Player once. And during that same time, the Dodgers won three National League pennants.

Of all the first basemen I've seen—guys like Keith Hernandez, who knew the game very well and always seemed to be in the right place, Andres Galarraga, and a few others whose names escape me right now—probably the one who came closest to Gil Hodges defensively was **Wes Parker**. And Gil worked with Parker in the Los Angeles Coliseum when Parker was a ballboy for the Dodgers. Gil would work with him at first base and show him some of the tricks of playing the position.

Parker was a left-handed thrower, which is a tremendous advantage for a first baseman, especially in making the first-short-first double play. And that's why, for me, Hodges is in a class by himself because he was a right-handed thrower.

In 1965 and 1966 Parker was part of the only all-switch-hitting infield in baseball history, with Jim Lefebvre at second, Maury Wills at short, and Jim Gilliam at third.

Wes wasn't a big power hitter at a position in which most teams want power. He hit only 64 home runs in his nine years, never more than 13 in any one season, and drove in more than 68 runs in a season just once. He had one big season in 1970, when he batted .319, drove in 111 runs, and led the National League with 47 doubles.

But he was a consistent .270 to .280 hitter, and his defense was superb. He won six consecutive Gold Gloves and had a lifetime fielding average of .996. In 1968 he made only one error, and that came in Houston on an AstroTurf bounce. The Dodgers writers later told Wes that it should have been a hit, but Houston's official scorer had been drinking.

Parker played only nine seasons in the major leagues and retired at the age of 32. He could have continued playing, but Wes is a very intelligent fellow with a wide variety of interests, and he apparently felt there was more to life than playing baseball.

He once admitted to me that he had a tough time committing himself to baseball. He liked to dabble in the stock market and to play in bridge tournaments. And he was a handsome, eligible bachelor who was a celebrity in

Wes Parker slides safely into third base during the 1965 World Series against the Minnesota Twins at Dodger Stadium. *Photo courtesy of Focus on Sport/Getty Images.*

Hollywood. Baseball often took a backseat to some of his other activities, and when he found he just couldn't give himself over to baseball as much as was necessary to maintain the high level he was playing at, he just walked away from the game and never looked back.

If I were picking the all-time Baltimore Orioles team, **Eddie Murray** would be number one at first base, hands down. But he played for the Dodgers for only three seasons, so I can't rate him higher than fifth, but I can't ignore him altogether either.

In his three years in Los Angeles, 1989 to 1991, Murray hit 20, 26, and 19 home runs; drove in 88, 95, and 96 runs; and had batting averages of .247, .330, and .260. To give the man his proper due, you have to look at his entire 21-season career, during which he had a lifetime batting average of .287, 504 home runs, and 1,917 RBIs and was elected to the Hall of Fame.

Like Parker, Murray was a switch-hitter, and if you were to put together an all-time switch-hitting team, Eddie would no doubt be the first baseman. Defensively, Murray wasn't a great first baseman, but he worked hard to make himself into a good one, good enough to win three Gold Gloves.

Eddie was one of the most perplexing individuals I have met in my years in baseball. He was an enigma. When I was a broadcaster in Montreal, I tried interviewing him a couple times and he always turned me down. Then I'd see him at a card show in the winter, and he'd come up to me and put his arm around me all buddy-buddy, and I'd say, "Aren't you the same guy that turned me down for an interview in Dodger Stadium?"

He'd say, "I don't do interviews."

"Hey," I'd say. "I've got a job to do too."

I'd walk out on the field and see him, and I'd say, "Hi, Eddie," and he'd walk past me like I wasn't there. He wouldn't even say hello to me when I was a broadcaster, but at a card show he was like my long lost buddy.

That's Eddie Murray. An enigma. But he could hit.

Although he doesn't make my top five at first base, I want to make special mention here of **Ron Fairly**, a good friend and a good major league player who had almost 2,000 major league hits, but less than half of them as a Dodger, where he played almost as many games in the outfield as he did at

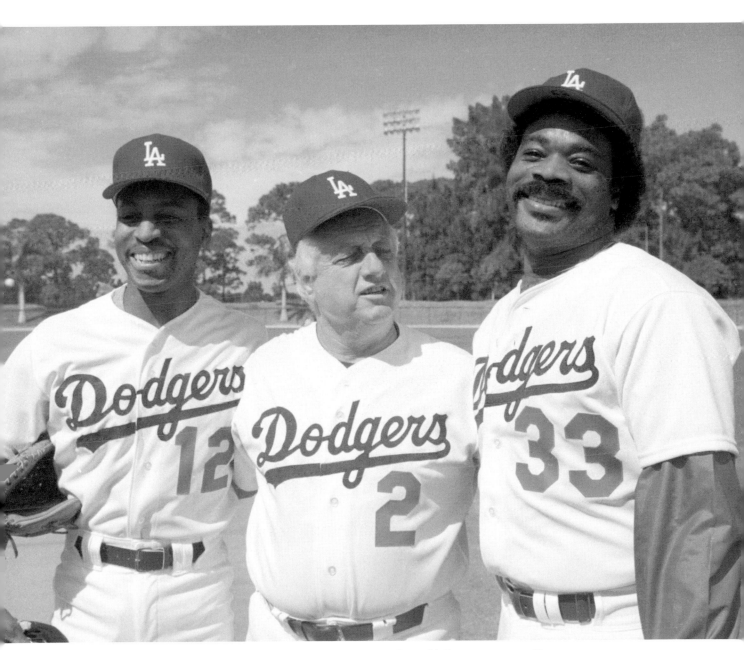

Eddie Murray (right) flashes a smile for the camera as he and fellow newcomer Willie Randolph (left) pose with manager Tommy Lasorda in 1989 in Vero Beach, Florida.

first base. Ron got the most out of his ability and was a good team player, and a delightful guy with a wonderful sense of humor.

One time he hit a ball in Dodger Stadium that was caught at the fence. When he came back to the bench, he said, "That's me, warning-track power. Even in Little League I had warning-track power."

By the way, that guy with "warning-track power" hit 215 home runs in his big-league career.

Statistical Summaries

All statistics are for player's Dodgers career only.

HITTING

G = Games

H = Hits

HR = Home runs

RBI = Runs batted in

SB = Stolen bases

BA = Batting average

First Baseman	Years	G	H	HR	RBI	SB	BA
Gil Hodges *Homered in five of the seven World Series he appeared in*	1943 1947–61	2,006	1,884	361	1,254	63	.274
Dolph Camilli *Averaged 148 games played during first five seasons as a Dodger*	1938–43	744	809	139	572	31	.270
Steve Garvey *Hit .392 in 10 All-Star Games*	1969–82	1,727	1,968	211	992	77	.301

continued	Years	G	H	HR	RBI	SB	BA
Wes Parker *Hit for the cycle at New York on May 7, 1970*	1964–72	1,288	1,110	64	470	60	.267
Eddie Murray *Averaged 93 RBIs during his Dodgers career*	1989–91	468	481	65	279	25	.278

FIELDING

PO = Putouts

A = Assists

E = Errors

DP = Double plays

TC/G = Total chances divided by games played

FA = Fielding average

First Baseman	PO	A	E	DP	TC/G	FA
Gil Hodges	14,968	1,241	121	1,584	8.8	.993
Dolph Camilli	7,736	546	71	660	10.0	.992
Steve Garvey	13,984	734	63	1,070	10.1	.996
Wes Parker	9,640	695	45	757	9.4	.996
Eddie Murray	3,823	378	23	306	9.2	.995

THREE

Second Baseman

I consider myself privileged to have been an eyewitness to history. I was there in Ebbets Field on April 15, 1947, sitting on the bench and getting paid to watch **Jackie Robinson** make his major league debut and break baseball's long-standing color barrier. I had also come up that season as a kid of 20 years, and I made my major league debut two days later. I pinch hit for Dixie Walker in the sixth inning of a one-sided game, got a base hit, and then went in and finished the game in right field. I would get into only 40 games and get 83 at-bats that season as an extra outfielder.

As I mentioned earlier, Jackie Robinson, seven years my senior, was no stranger to me. I remembered him as a four-sport star back home at Pasadena Junior College and was so impressed by his athletic ability that he became one of my early idols. Then, just six years later, I was his teammate and a witness to history.

1. JACKIE ROBINSON

2. JIM GILLIAM

3. DAVEY LOPES

4. BILLY HERMAN

5. EDDIE STANKY

I can't say that we were very close or that we were even friends that first year. I was a rookie, just a kid, and he was a mature man who had enough on his plate, was under such pressure to succeed that he didn't have time to

33

The legendary Jackie Robinson safely steals home plate ahead of the tag by Boston Braves catcher Bill Salkeld at Ebbets Field on August 22, 1948.

bother with me. I didn't even belong there. I had been in the navy and, at the time, if a returning serviceman made the team, he had to be kept with the big club until a year after his discharge date. So, the Dodgers were stuck with me for half a season, and I got to see firsthand, but from afar, what Robinson went through.

I saw a man driven to excel, a man with the weight of an entire race on his shoulders. If he failed, it would set the whole experiment back years, even decades. I can't imagine trying to perform under such scrutiny and such pressure.

How he was able to play, and to play at such a high level, I can't even imagine, but he did. I dressed a few lockers away from him, and I could see the anguish on his face, the frustration, and the anger. You could see the fire in his eyes. He wasn't saying anything that first year—he kept it all inside—but you could just tell it was eating him up.

I firmly believe that Jackie is the only person—not the only black person, the only person—I have known that could have handled the situation he was put in. That's how much inner strength Jackie had.

On the field I heard the taunts and the insults from players on other teams, and even from fans when we were on the road. Almost daily, I saw fans throw things at him, players go out of their way to try to spike him, pitchers throw at his head. One day a fan let a black cat loose on the field. There were even death threats.

Rival players weren't his only tormentors. Some of his own teammates were his enemies. They isolated him, refused to talk to him, and circulated a petition among the team stating their objection to playing with a man of color. Because I was just a rookie I was never asked to sign the petition, and I'm glad I wasn't. I wouldn't have signed it anyway.

After I got to know Jackie and what a fierce competitor he was, I reflected on that first year and came to the conclusion that it must have eaten at his insides not to retaliate. He had promised Branch Rickey that he would take whatever taunts, insults, and physical abuse was handed to him and turn the other cheek because to fight back would have set back the whole movement. Jackie kept his word that first year.

I firmly believe that Jackie is the only person —not the only *black* person, the only *person*—I have known that could have handled the situation he was put in. I don't know of anybody who could have handled it as well as Jackie handled it, and that's a broad statement because I've come across a lot of fine people. That's how much inner strength Jackie had.

Through all the opposition, Robinson performed courageously and skillfully. The Dodgers already had Eddie Stanky at second base, so they put Robinson at first base, a position that was strange to him. Nevertheless, he became a more than adequate first baseman.

Offensively, he was a force and a catalyst. He would do whatever it took to win a game. He would bunt his way on, challenge outfielders' arms by taking an extra base, and disrupt defenses and unnerve pitchers by stealing a base. He led the league with 29 stolen bases, had 175 hits, scored 125 runs, hit 12 home runs, drove in 48 runs out of the number two batting position, batted .297, and was named Rookie of the Year.

35

To say that Jackie Robinson was one of the most important figures in the history of baseball is a gross understatement. He was much more than that: one of the most important figures in American history, a civil rights advocate on equal footing with Abraham Lincoln, Martin Luther King Jr., Harry Truman, John and Bobby Kennedy, and Rosa Parks. The fact that he was a baseball player, and an exceptionally good one, is merely incidental.

Almost 60 years after he broke baseball's color barrier, Jackie Robinson's legacy lives on in the wondrous diamond deeds of Ken Griffey Jr., Barry Bonds, David Ortiz, Dontrelle Willis, and Gary Sheffield, and in the dugouts where Frank Robinson, Dusty Baker, and Willie Randolph hold forth.

He was many things to many people: a savior, a pioneer, a trailblazer, an uncompromising competitor, an irritant to opponents, an inspiration, a hero, and, above all, a winner. The following statements illustrate how Jackie Robinson is viewed by teammates, opponents, statesmen, and his descendants.

Branch Rickey: "There was never a man in the game who could put mind and muscle together quicker and with better judgment than Jackie Robinson."

Rickey to Robinson: "Jackie, we've got no army. There's virtually nobody on our side. No owners, no umpires, very few newspapermen. And I'm afraid that many fans will be hostile. We'll be in a tough position. We can win only if we can convince the world that I'm doing this because you're a great ballplayer, and a fine gentleman."

Carl Erskine: "Jackie needed to quell his anger the first couple of years, a task which only someone of his inner strength and vision could have coped with at that moment [in time]. When I reflect and wonder what it must have been like for a man who should have been at the happiest moments in his life to still have to deal with racial indignities on a daily basis, it is mind-boggling. Most mortal men would have cracked."

Pee Wee Reese: "I don't know any other ballplayer who could have done what he did—to be able to hit with everybody yelling at him. He had to block all that out, block out everything but the ball coming in at 100 miles per hour. To do what he did has got to be the most tremendous thing I've ever seen in sports."

Bob Gibson: "If I were in Jackie Robinson's shoes, I probably never would have made it."

Ralph Kiner: "Jackie Robinson was the best athlete ever to play major league baseball."

Joe Black: "All of us had to wait for Jackie."

Willie Mays: "Every time I look at my pocketbook, I see Jackie Robinson."

Charlie Dressen: "Give me five players like Jackie Robinson and a pitcher and I'll beat any nine-man team in baseball."

Leo Durocher: "I don't care if the guy is yellow or black, or if he has stripes like a bleeping zebra. I'm the manager of this team, and I say he plays."

Red Schoendienst: "If it wasn't for him, the Dodgers would be in the second division."

Bobby Bragan: "He was the only player I ever saw in a rundown who could be safe more often than out. He ran as if his head was on a swizzle, back and forth, back and forth, until he could get out of it."

Mickey Mantle: "After the game [Game 7 of the 1952 World Series], Jackie Robinson came into our clubhouse and shook my hand. He said, 'You're a helluva player, and you've got a great future.' I thought that was a classy gesture, one I wasn't then capable of making. I was a bad loser. What meant even more was what Jackie told the press: 'Mantle beat us. He was the difference between the two teams. They didn't miss DiMaggio.' I have to admit, I became a Jackie Robinson fan on the spot. And when I think of that World Series, his gesture comes to mind. Here was a player who had without a doubt suffered more abuse and more taunts and more hatred than any player in the history of the game. And he had made a special effort to compliment and encourage a young white kid from Oklahoma."

President Ronald Reagan: "He struck a mighty blow for equality, freedom, and the American way of life. Jackie Robinson was a good citizen, a great man, and a true American champion."

Jesse Jackson: "He was a therapist for the masses by succeeding, by doing it with such style, flair, and drama. He helped level baseball off, to make it truly a game for black and white, with excellence the only test for success."

Henry Aaron: "I was 14 years old when I first saw Jackie Robinson. It was the spring of 1948, the year after Jackie changed my life by breaking baseball's color line. His team, the Brooklyn Dodgers, made a stop in my hometown of

Mobile, Alabama, while barnstorming its way north to start the season, and while he was there, Jackie spoke to a big crowd of black folks over on Davis Avenue. I think he talked about segregation, but I didn't hear a word that came out of his mouth. Jackie Robinson was such a hero to me that I couldn't do anything but gawk at him.

"They say certain people are bigger than life, but Jackie Robinson is the only man I've known who truly was. In 1947 life in America—at least my America and Jackie's—was segregation. It was two worlds that were afraid of each other. There were separate schools for blacks and whites, separate restaurants, separate hotels, separate drinking fountains, and separate baseball leagues. Life was unkind to black people who tried to bring those worlds together. It could be hateful. But Jackie Robinson, God bless him, was bigger than all of that."

Jackie Robinson on Jackie Robinson: "Above everything else, I hate to lose. It kills me to lose. If I'm a troublemaker, and I don't think that my temper makes me one, then it's because I can't stand losing. That's the way I am about winning. All I ever wanted to do was finish first."

"Baseball is like a poker game. Nobody wants to quit when he's losing; nobody wants you to quit when you're ahead."

"I'm not concerned with you liking me or disliking me. All I ask is that you respect me as a human being."

"A life is not important except in the impact it has on other lives."

By the way he played and the way he conducted himself, Jackie showed everyone that he belonged and why Rickey chose him, why he was the right man at the right time. We won the pennant in his first year by five games over the Cardinals, and we certainly would not have won it without Robinson. The irony is that those players who circulated the petition benefited by collecting a World Series check they probably would not have received were it not for the man they didn't want as a teammate.

The following year Stanky was traded to the Boston Braves, and that opened up second base for Jackie. As a side benefit, it also opened up first base for Gil Hodges.

I was Jackie's teammate for the next nine seasons. We also became friends. I watched him bat over .300 six straight years, win a batting title with a .342

average, drive in 124 runs, be named Most Valuable Player in 1949, and score more than 100 runs six out of his first seven years (the one year he failed to score 100, he fell one run short). In Jackie's 10 years in Brooklyn, we won six pennants, and he was a major contributor to all of them.

I also saw the wraps come off him and watched him fight back. He had taken so much, and then he began to give it back. And, believe me, he could dish it out. He was fierce and he was mean; he was sarcastic and he was caustic.

I was embarrassed by the way he was treated when he first came up. And I was somewhat embarrassed by some of the things he later did or said in retribution. Then I would think back and remember what he had gone through, and I'd say, "Hey, he didn't do anything then." I know I wouldn't have been able to handle it, so I figured he earned the right to do and say those things.

The whole idea of racism was completely foreign to me and contrary to my upbringing. I didn't grow up with any thoughts that one race was better than another. There were black families in my neighborhood in California, and I went to school with African-American kids and played on teams with them in high school, so to me there was nothing unusual about playing alongside a black man.

My first real taste of racism came when I signed a professional baseball contract. I was 17 years old, and I went off to play in Newport News, Virginia. It was there that I first saw drinking fountains and rest rooms labeled for "whites" and for "colored," and segregated seating on public transportation.

One day I climbed onto a bus and went immediately to the back, as I always did. I preferred to sit in the backs of buses, airplanes, and trains. When I took my seat, I got strange looks from the black folks and dirty looks from the whites. I didn't realize I was sitting in the black section. I didn't know any better. We didn't have those sections in California.

Even later, in the fifties, I still encountered racism. There were some cities, like St. Louis, Cincinnati, and even Philadelphia, where the black players could not stay at the same hotel as the rest of us. So they stayed either at a hotel in the black section of town or with friends in private homes. Even when the hotels opened their doors to the black players, they were not allowed to eat in the hotel dining room.

Florida in those days was especially difficult for the black players. We'd take long bus trips to play exhibition games and we'd stop to eat, and Jackie, Campy, and Newk would have to stay in the bus while the rest of us went inside. Somebody would get them their food and bring it out to them, and they'd eat on the bus.

Some of the veteran white guys, led by Carl Erskine, who was our player representative, complained about this policy. Erskine went to our traveling secretary Lee Scott and said, "Find a place that will take the whole team, or we won't stop."

Because of the humiliation he suffered from having to eat on the bus, Jackie stopped riding the bus to exhibition games and had a friend drive him instead.

Later, when the hotels permitted the black players to eat in the hotel dining room, there would be times when a few of us would be seated and in would walk Campy and Newk, and we'd invite them to join us. Or, if they were already seated, we'd go to their table and plop ourselves down with them. I never did see Jackie in the hotel dining room. It may have been his silent protest at being denied admittance in the past; in any case, he would either get room service or eat at friends' homes. Perhaps he didn't like to socialize, or maybe he didn't want to cause the white players any uneasiness, but I never saw him in the hotel dining room.

In fact, I can't remember ever sharing a meal with Jackie, except for one time. After the 1956 World Series, we went to Japan to play a series of exhibition games against Japanese teams. One night Bev and I and Carl Erskine and his wife, Betty, were on our way to a local restaurant for dinner. In the lobby we ran into Rachel and Jackie Robinson.

"Where are you folks going?" Jackie asked.

"We're going to a restaurant up the street for dinner," Erskine said. "Why don't you join us?"

Jackie looked at Rachel and, almost shyly, Rachel looked at Jackie, shrugged, and said, "Why not?"

We wound up having a wonderful night. Rachel was charming, and Jackie was great company. I saw a side of Jackie I had rarely ever seen. He was relaxed and talkative. We laughed a lot and had an enjoyable evening, and I couldn't help wondering why we didn't do it more often.

Jackie wasn't the fastest player on the Dodgers, but he was a great and daring base runner, a gambler. He was pigeon-toed and looked awkward when he ran, but he was so daring on the bases that he could disrupt a defense and unnerve a pitcher. He was a constant threat as a base stealer, and he had a way of taunting pitchers and catchers by dancing off the bases. They had to be aware of him, which often broke the pitcher's concentration and gave the hitter a big advantage.

Jack took chances others might not have. He had great quickness, if not speed (he never stole more than 37 bases in any of his 10 seasons), and tremendous instincts for the game and the situation. He knew when to take the extra base and when not to, when to steal and when not to

In the eighth inning of the first game of the 1955 World Series, with the Yankees leading 6–4, Robinson, by then past his prime, surprised everyone by stealing home. To this day, Yogi Berra insists Jackie was out. To this day, we believe he was safe—and he was. We wound up losing that game 6–5, but winning the World Series four games to three.

Robinson became a master at taunting and intimidation, not only with his bat, his glove, his arm, and his legs, but also with his head and his mouth.

One day in Chicago I was hitting against "Toothpick" Sam Jones, and I heard a voice coming from behind me: "I'm going to get you, Sam. Just wait until I get in that batter's box."

It was Jackie, yelling at Jones from the on-deck circle.

I flied out, and Jackie stepped into the batter's box, still jabbering away.

"C'mon, Sam," he said. "Throw that thing in here so I can do something with it, unless you're afraid to."

Jones was so unnerved that he hit Jackie with a pitch—maybe accidentally, maybe not. That was just what Jackie wanted. He was on base, and he continued to give it to Sam, who tried to pick Jackie off first and threw the ball wildly down the right-field line. Robinson raced all the way to third.

Then Jackie started dancing off third, as only he could, still yelling at Jones.

"Look out, Sam, I'm going to steal home. Get ready, because I'm going."

He would have too, but he didn't have to. He had ruined Jones' concentration so that Sam bounced a curveball on the next pitch, the ball got past the catcher, Jackie trotted home, and we beat the Cubs by one run.

Another time, we were playing the Giants, and there was a story in one of the newspapers that quoted Tom Sheehan, the Giants' scout, saying, "Carl Erskine's pitching against us tomorrow. He's over the hill. He can't get anybody out. We'll beat him."

Jackie got two copies of the article. He gave one to Erskine, and the other he put in his pocket. Erskine beat the Giants that day, and when the game was over, Jackie went over to the Giants' box behind the visitor's dugout in Ebbets Field where Sheehan was sitting, took the article out of his pocket, handed it to Sheehan, and said, "Here, put this in your mouth and chew on it."

Jackie was the greatest competitor I have ever seen on a baseball field. He hated to lose and he would do anything to beat you—and I mean anything.

Late in his career he was plagued with bad knees. His competitive desire was still there, as was much of his talent, but he could hardly run. It was painful to watch him, and considering what he had once been, it also was sad.

In 1956 he played in only 117 games, and his average dropped to .275. After the season, he was traded to the Giants, but Jackie refused to report. He could have taken the money, maybe played another year or two, but he retired instead. I think he was hurt that the Dodgers would trade him. I also believe that he couldn't bear the thought of wearing the uniform of the Dodgers' most hated rivals.

Jim Gilliam joined the Dodgers in 1953 and made an immediate impact on the team. To make room for Gilliam at second base, Jackie Robinson was shifted to left field and then to third base, and those moves improved us defensively and offensively.

Jackie was getting older, and he was having trouble with his knees, which affected his mobility. Third base is a more stationary position and not as stressful on the legs. So the change improved our defense. And it also improved our offense. Removed from the burden of playing second base, Jackie raised his average from .308 to .329 and his runs batted in from 75 to 95. And Gilliam gave our offense a jump start by providing us with the kind of leadoff batter we hadn't had in years. He had 168 hits and 100 walks, scored 125 runs and drove in 63, led the league with 17 triples, stole 21 bases, and was named National League Rookie of the Year.

Gilliam was a delightful fellow, a great guy to be around. Fans knew him as Jim or Junior, but around the players, his nickname was "the Devil." We called him "the Devil" because one day Jim, who was a very good pool player, went into a poolroom in Vero Beach, Florida, threw a couple hundred-dollar bills down, and said, "Anybody want a part of the Devil?" And from that day on, he was "the Devil."

When Gilliam joined us in the spring of 1953, he said, "Boy, I'm really happy to get a chance to play on this team. I like to run. I'll get on base, and you guys knock me in."

Jim Gilliam, who was a valuable offensive weapon at the leadoff spot and a versatile defensive player, takes some cuts at Ebbets Field in 1953, his first season as a Dodger. *Photo courtesy of Diamond Images/Getty Images.*

43

In June we were standing around the batting cage at Ebbets Field, and Jim said, "I got to get a day off. I've lost five pounds already this season, and I don't have any weight to lose (Gilliam weighed only about 170 pounds). I'm getting tired."

He was going from first to third, from first to home, scoring all those runs. I told him, "You said you wanted to run; well, we're running you."

Jim was great for a ballclub. He never complained. He wanted to play every day, and he went out and played hard. He didn't make the double play all that well, and he didn't have a really strong arm, but he was a sure-handed fielder, he knew the game, and he got on base and scored runs.

Gilliam was an outstanding offensive ballplayer and a versatile one on defense. You could put him just about anywhere on the field and he'd do a good job. He wound up playing more than 1,000 games at second base, more than 700 at third base (I'll talk about Gilliam as a third baseman in the chapter on third basemen), and more than 200 games in the outfield. He even played two games at first base.

What a lot of people forget is that he started in left field for us and Don Zimmer started at second base in the seventh game of the 1955 World Series. In the sixth inning George Shuba pinch hit for Zimmer, and in the bottom of the inning Gilliam moved from left field to second base and Sandy Amoros went in to play left field. And, of course, it was in that inning that Amoros made his great, game-saving catch of Yogi Berra's high-twisting drive down the left-field line and then turned and doubled Gil McDougald at first.

Chances are, Gilliam would not have made that catch. For one thing, he wasn't as experienced an outfielder as Amoros was, and for another, Gilliam was a right-handed thrower and Amoros was left-handed. That meant Sandy had his glove on his right hand, closer to the foul line, which enabled him to make that catch. A right-handed outfielder, with the glove on his left hand—closer to center field—might not have reached the ball.

Gilliam scored more than 100 runs in each of his first four seasons. He wound up playing 14 seasons (all with the Dodgers), scored more than 1,100 runs, had almost 1,900 hits, and stole more than 200 bases.

After the 1964 season Gilliam retired, and Walter Alston made him the Dodgers' third-base coach. But when an infield emergency arose, Jim came out of retirement and played third base on the only all-switch-hitting infield in baseball history—Wes Parker at first, Jim Lefebvre at second, Maury Wills at short, and Gilliam at third.

In 111 games Gilliam batted .280 and helped the Dodgers win the World Series against the Twins. He retired again after the 1965 season but came back again for 88 games and another National League pennant in 1966, before finally retiring for good and returning to the coaching staff.

Gilliam was the Dodgers' good-luck charm, and he became one of the most popular figures ever to wear the Los Angeles Dodgers uniform. Tragically, just before the start of the 1978 World Series, Jim suffered a brain hemorrhage and died. He was only 50 years old.

Davey Lopes was part of the longest-running infield in baseball history—Steve Garvey at first, Lopes at second, Bill Russell at short, and Ron Cey at third. The four played together for nine seasons, longer than any other infield ever. Together, they won four pennants and one World Series.

I'm proud to say that two of those four infielders, Russell and Lopes, began their professional careers as center fielders, which proves the point that you have to be a good athlete to play center field.

I liked the way Lopes played the game. He knew what his job was as the leadoff hitter: get on base, steal bases, score runs, play good defense, play every day. In six of those nine seasons, Davey played more than 140 games.

Lopes was a good, solid ballplayer, both offensively and defensively, but he probably will be best remembered as one of the premier base stealers of his time. He stole 36 bases or more in seven straight seasons, once stole five bases in a game to tie a 70-year-old National League record, and at one point set a major league record with 38 consecutive successful steals.

Davey Lopes, who started his career as a center fielder, was part of the longest-running infield in baseball history. *Photo courtesy of MLB Photos/Getty Images.*

I heard a lot about **Billy Herman** from Pee Wee Reese. Pee Wee and I used to drive to Ebbets Field together every day, and we'd talk about baseball all the time. He would tell me about players he played with that I never saw, like Dolph Camilli, Pete Reiser, and Billy Herman.

I learned from Pee Wee that Herman was a great baseball man, a great hit-and-run man, and a great team player. I heard nothing but great things about him. He was the perfect number two hitter in the batting order: excellent at hitting behind the runner, willing to give himself up to move a runner along, and very unselfish.

William Jennings Bryan Herman was a little short on speed, I guess, but he covered the ground, made the double play really well, and knew the game. When he got a little older, he relied on his knowledge to position himself for hitters. In other words, he played the game the way it's supposed to be played.

Billy Herman's best years were as a Chicago Cub, but he came over to Brooklyn in 1941 and made a winning double-play combination with shortstop Pee Wee Reese.

Kirby Higbe, a teammate of Herman's with the Cubs and Dodgers, once said, "[Herman] stood out at second base over any other second baseman I ever saw. He was the greatest hit-and-run man in baseball, then or now." And Leo Durocher called Herman "the classic number two hitter, an absolute master at hitting behind the runner."

Herman had his best years with the Cubs. Six times he batted over .300. In 1935 he led the National League in hits with 227 and in doubles with 57, batted .341, and scored 113 runs. In 1939 he led the league with 18 triples. All of which eventually got him elected to the Hall of Fame.

When he got off to a slow start in 1941, Herman was traded to the Dodgers, although it's been said that the real reason for the trade was not his slow start but because Cubs manager Jimmie Wilson saw Herman as a threat to his job.

"[Herman] stood out at second base over any other second baseman I ever saw. He was the greatest hit-and-run man in baseball, then or now."

—KIRBY HIGBE

In Brooklyn Durocher put Herman in the number two spot in the batting order, behind Reese. Billy batted .291, drove in 41 runs, and scored 77 runs in 133 games and teamed with Reese at shortstop to give the Dodgers a solid double-play combination that was largely responsible for them winning their first pennant in 21 years.

Because of his baseball intelligence, everybody thought Herman would make a great manager. He got his shot with the Pittsburgh Pirates in 1947, but Billy wasn't ready for the job. He couldn't handle the guys in Pittsburgh; they were a party crew.

After 17 years Billy got another chance to manage, this time with the Red Sox. Again he was a disappointing failure. In two seasons he was 126–182 and didn't finish higher than ninth. He never managed again, but he did stay in the game as a coach and scout.

I'm not going to sugarcoat this. I never liked **Eddie Stanky**. He wasn't one of my favorite people, as an opponent or as a teammate. I don't think he was a very nice man. But I had great respect for him. He played the game hard and he played it well, and you can't let personal feelings enter into your judgment.

When I came up to the Dodgers in 1947, Stanky was the second baseman. I wasn't a regular player, and I had only three bats. It's not like today when players have two or three dozen bats. I had only three, and I didn't like to use

Eddie Stanky (second from right) was the Dodgers' second baseman when Jackie
Robinson (right) came up and broke the color barrier. Robinson played first base until
Stanky was traded to make room for the new superstar. Also pictured are Spider Jorgensen
(left) and Pee Wee Reese.

my bat in batting practice because if I broke it, I might not have a bat if I had to pinch hit.

One day during batting practice, I picked up one of Stanky's bats. It was lying there, a batting-practice bat, so I used it. Stanky came up to the batting cage and said, "Whose bat you got?"

"Yours," I said.

"Give me that damn bat," he said "You're not supposed to use my bat for batting practice."

He started giving me a lot of static, and Pee Wee said, "Here, Duke, use mine." Then Pee Wee took Stanky aside and said something to him, I don't know what. It was like I was a rookie and I didn't even belong there. It ticked me off, and I never liked Stanky after that.

Years later, when Stanky was managing the Cardinals, I had a couple hits in a game, and he called timeout and brought in a left-hander, Royce Lint, to pitch to me. As Stanky went back to the dugout, he looked at me and said in that sarcastic way of his, "Let's see how you hit off this guy." I hit a triple off the center-field fence. Then a pitch got by the catcher, the catcher threw the ball to Lint covering home plate, and I kicked the ball out of Lint's glove and scored. I got up at home plate and looked at Stanky in the Cardinals dugout and made a gesture that I won't get into here.

What they used to say about me was, "Don't wake him up. You might get him out, but when you do, leave him alone."

I was a guy who liked to talk to other players, even opponents. But when Stanky was with the Giants, I never even said hello to him. I didn't like him. He tried to pattern himself after Leo Durocher.

I didn't like Stanky, but as I said, I respected him as a ballplayer. They called him "the Brat," and that describes the kind of player he was. He was always in your hair, making mischief. He'd do anything to beat you, and not all of it was within the rules. Stanky got more out of his ability than almost anybody else would have. He could foul a ball off, peck away, and get on base. As a player, he was a winner.

I remember a game in Cincinnati in 1947 when Ewell Blackwell was pitching against us for the Reds and going after his second-consecutive no-hitter, which, of course, had been done only once before in baseball history, by Johnny Vander Meer, also with Cincinnati, nine years earlier.

We went to the ninth inning without a hit. Gene Hermanski pinch hit to lead off the inning and flied out to left. That brought up Stanky, and we could

*It just seemed like good teams followed
Stanky around.*

see the determination on his face. He was damned if
Blackwell was going to pitch a no-hitter against us.
And Stanky hit one right through Blackwell's legs
into center field and broke up the no-hitter. That's
the kind of competitor he was.

It was Stanky who prompted Leo Durocher to make his famous remark
that "nice guys finish last." The story goes that Leo was talking to reporters
one day and said, "Look at Mel Ott over there [sitting in the Giants dugout].
He's a nice guy, and he finishes second. Now look at the Brat [Stanky]. He
can't hit, can't run, can't field. He's no nice guy, but all the little SOB can do
is win."

Stanky came up with the Cubs and was traded to the Dodgers during the
1944 season. The following year, he drew a team-record 148 walks and led
the National League with 128 runs scored. In 1947, when Jackie Robinson
arrived in Brooklyn, Stanky was the second baseman, so Jackie played first
base, and the Dodgers won the pennant.

I will say this about Stanky. He was one of the first Dodgers to stick up for
Robinson. Early in the 1947 season the Dodgers played a series in Philadelphia. The Phillies and their manager, Ben Chapman, were particularly
vicious in their remarks toward Jackie, calling him "shoe-shine boy," "nig-
ger," and "black SOB."

Stanky, who was from Alabama, heard these insults coming from the
Phillies dugout, looked into the dugout, and shouted, "Listen, you cowards,
why don't you yell at somebody who can fight back?"

The following year, Stanky was traded to Boston to open up second base
for Robinson. With Stanky, the Braves won the pennant in 1948. Two years
later he and Alvin Dark were traded to the Giants, and they won the pennant
in 1951. It just seemed like good teams followed Stanky around.

He played 11 years in the big leagues, batted .268, hit 29 home runs, drove
in 364 runs, stole 48 bases, and had a fielding percentage of .975.

It's like Durocher said, "He can't hit, can't run, can't field. All the little
SOB can do is win."

Statistical Summaries

All statistics are for player's Dodgers career only.

HITTING

G = Games

H = Hits

HR = Home runs

RBI = Runs batted in

SB = Stolen bases

BA = Batting average

Second Baseman	Years	G	H	HR	RBI	SB	BA
Jackie Robinson *Stole home 19 times in his career*	1947–56	1,382	1,518	137	734	197	.311
Jim Gilliam *Set NL record for rookies with 100 walks in 1953*	1953–66	1,956	1,889	65	558	203	.265
Davey Lopes *Stole five bases on August 24, 1974, tying then-NL record*	1972–81	1,207	1,204	99	384	418	.262

continued	Years	G	H	HR	RBI	SB	BA
Billy Herman *Led NL in games played, with 154, in 1943*	1941–43 1946	488	548	7	234	13	.292
Eddie Stanky *Led NL in walks three times, twice with Dodgers (1945 and 1946)*	1944–47	532	488	4	144	20	.263

FIELDING

PO = Putouts

A = Assists

E = Errors

DP = Double plays

TC/G = Total chances divided by games played

FA = Fielding average

Second Baseman	PO	A	E	DP	TC/G	FA
Jackie Robinson	1,877	2,047	68	607	5.3	.983
Jim Gilliam	2,279	2,724	107	628	4.9	.979
Davey Lopes	2,578	3,174	135	639	5.1	.977
Billy Herman	1,013	1,114	60	235	5.2	.973
Eddie Stanky	1,319	1,344	74	340	5.5	.973

FOUR

Shortstop

To me, and to about 100 others who wore the Dodgers uniform in the forties and fifties, **Pee Wee Reese** is, was, and always will be Mr. Dodger, just as Ernie Banks is Mr. Cub.

Don't be misled by the nickname. Pee Wee wasn't a little guy, as his name implies. He stood 5'10" and weighed about 175 pounds. He was solidly built and strong. He picked up his nickname when, as a kid, he won a marble championship in his native Louisville, Kentucky—a peewee is a type of marble. The nickname stuck with him for life, and it even became a term of endearment.

He wasn't the biggest Dodger, or the fastest, or the strongest. He didn't hit the most home runs or have the

1. Pee Wee Reese

2. Bill Russell

3. Maury Wills

4. Leo Durocher

5. Lonny Frey

highest batting average or steal the most bases, but, for my money, he was the greatest Dodger of them all: a great shortstop, a great leader, a great team player, and a great mentor and friend. He was the consummate professional. I learned so much from Pee Wee. He was "the Little Colonel" out of Louisville, Kentucky. He was our captain, and he would remain our captain forever. Years after he quit playing, he was still our captain.

Pee Wee Reese slides safely home ahead of the throw in a game against the Cubs at Ebbets Field in 1942.

With the possible exception of Gil Hodges, Reese was the most beloved of the so-called Boys of Summer, and the fans of Brooklyn demonstrated that love on a memorable night in 1955. It was Pee Wee's 37th birthday, and the Dodgers threw him a birthday party in Ebbets Field. He was showered with gifts before the game, but the highlight of the night came in the fifth inning. They dimmed the lights, and thirty-five thousand fans lit candles and serenaded "the Captain" by singing "Happy Birthday." The whole thing sent chills down my spine.

The Dodgers got lucky in getting Reese, who had signed with the Boston Red Sox. At the time Joe Cronin, a great player who would go to the Hall of Fame, was the manager and shortstop in Boston. Cronin was getting older, and Reese was considered his eventual replacement. But Cronin was reluctant to give up his position and more than willing to approve the sale of Reese's contract to the Dodgers.

Pee Wee arrived in Brooklyn in 1940 at the age of 21 and found himself in a situation similar to the one in Boston. The man playing his position was his manager, Leo Durocher. But unlike Cronin, Durocher knew his best days as a player were behind him and his future was as a manager, and he recognized that in Pee Wee he had a shortstop who would be productive for years to come. Leo willingly and eagerly turned his shortstop job over to Pee Wee. Except for the three years he took off for military service, Reese remained the Dodgers shortstop, and the heart and soul of the team, for the next 17 years.

In that time shortstops kept coming along to challenge Reese for the position. It seemed that every year there was some hotshot who was going to unseat Pee Wee as the Dodgers' shortstop, but none of them ever did until Pee Wee moved to third base in 1957. He was 39 years old at the time.

Of all the shortstops who the Dodgers groomed in the minor leagues for Pee Wee's job—someone once counted up the number and it came to 27, from Bobby Morgan to Chico Fernandez to Bob Ramazzotti to Tommy Brown to Eddie Miksis to Stan Rojek—the one who posed the most serious challenge was Don Zimmer. Pee Wee buried all the rest: some died in the minor leagues, some were traded, and some were sold. But I'll never forget standing with Pee Wee by the batting cage in spring training one day in 1953 watching a young Zimmer hit in batting practice. Pee Wee looked at me and said, "I might have to move to third base for this guy."

That was Don Zimmer—what a great-looking young player he was. He could hit, he had a gun for an arm, and he could run like a deer. He could do everything. The Dodgers sent him to St. Paul, Minnesota, in the American Association, and a few months later he was hitting .300 and leading the league in home runs and RBIs. Then he was hit in the head by a pitch. This was before they started using batting helmets. Zimmer was unconscious for almost two weeks, and when he regained consciousness he couldn't speak for another four weeks. He lost 44 pounds and had four screws inserted in his head.

After that his vision was blurred and he wasn't the same player because he couldn't see. He was almost blind in his left eye. Eventually the blurred vision cleared and Zim fought his way back. He was even our second baseman in the 1955 World Series, and then he was hit in the head again by a pitch early in the 1956 season. He had played in only 17 games and was batting .300 at the time. He missed the rest of that season and never was the same player again. But he wound up playing 12 years in the major leagues and then went on to be a coach and a manager, spending more than 60 years in baseball.

But let me tell you, he would have been one of the great players in the game had he not gotten hurt. He could play. Talk about ability, desire to play, and knowledge of the game—he had it all. I love that guy. He and I were buddies from the first day he put the uniform on.

I can't say that Zim would have taken Reese's shortstop job away from him, but the Dodgers would have had to make room for Zimmer *and* Reese. The great thing about Pee Wee is that he was a winner. It's no accident that the Dodgers won the pennant with Reese at shortstop in 1941, his rookie year, and that they won again in 1947, the year after he returned from the navy, and again in 1949, 1952, 1953, 1955, and 1956, all with Reese at shortstop.

When I first came up, Reese kind of took me under his wing, and after I'd been around a while, we lived close to each other in Brooklyn and rode back and forth to the ballpark every day together. We'd talk baseball all the time, about the game in general and our team in particular. And, because I was a Dodgers fan as a kid, I often asked Pee Wee about players I had read and heard about but never saw. He was my eyes and ears, and a great resource for me.

He also was a great help to me as a player. He knew when to pat me on the back, and he knew when to get on me and prod me to do better. I often batted right behind Reese in the lineup—he batted leadoff until Jim Gilliam came along, and then Pee Wee hit second and I batted third. He was an ideal number two man in a batting order, and I loved hitting behind him because he had a knack for getting on base. He gave me many opportunities to knock him in.

So spectacular was Marty Marion's defensive play at shortstop that in 1944 he was voted the Most Valuable Player in the National League although he only batted .267, hit six home runs, and drove in 63. He was Mr. Shortstop, the standard against which all shortstops were measured then (an era of great shortstops such as Joe Cronin, Luke Appling, Lou Boudreau, Phil Rizzuto, Arky Vaughan, Eddie Miller, and Pee Wee Reese) and for years to come.

At a time when shortstops generally were "little" guys—less than 6' tall—Marion was considered unorthodox. He was a gangly 6'4", 170 pounds, and all arms and legs, which earned him the nickname "the Octopus" and enabled him to cover acres of infield real estate and to gracefully suck up ground balls.

"I think I was the first tall shortstop," Marion said. "In my day, most shortstops were shorter guys like Reese and Rizzuto. Cecil Travis was about 6'1", but guys like us were rare. Today there are a lot of tall short-stops, and it's become an offensive position. Shortstops today are hit-ting 30, 40, 50 home runs. [Editor's note: Marion was never in double figures in home runs in any one season.] But everybody hits home runs today."

Marion's career with the St. Louis Cardinals overlapped Reese's with the Dodgers. In fact, they go back as rivals to their minor league days—Reese in Louisville, Marion in Rochester. They reached the major leagues in the same year, 1940, and for the next decade they were contemporaries, and rivals.

Marion remembers that time:

> In those days, it seems we were always battling the Dodgers for the pennant, and people were always comparing me and Reese. The Dodgers were our enemies. We hated them and they hated us, but it was nothing personal. It was just that we were fighting for the same prize.
>
> Pee Wee and I would talk as we passed each other on the field. He'd say, "I saw you hit a home run the other day," or I would com-pliment him on a play he had made. But we were opponents, and

we wanted to beat each other. I never knew him other than on the baseball field.

Pee Wee was a great shortstop—hard to beat him—a good, consistent shortstop who made all the routine plays and a good guy for a ballclub because he was so steady. And he was a leader. Every ballclub needs a leader, and Reese was the Dodgers' leader.

In the five-year period from 1946 to 1950, either Marion or Reese was the starting shortstop for the National League in the All-Star Games, Marion in 1946, 1947, and 1950, Reese in 1948 and 1949. While Reese was in the navy, Marion, who was deferred from military service because of a slipped disk in his back, was the National League's starting All-Star shortstop in 1943 and 1944.

There were no Gold Gloves awarded in his day. But had there been, Marion might have strung together 9 or 10 in succession, so dominant was his defense.

A chronic bad back curtailed Marion's career, and his mediocre offense (a lifetime average of .263, 36 career home runs, and 624 RBIs) probably prevented him from being elected to the Hall of Fame. Reese, on the other hand, played longer, had better offensive statistics (a .269 average, 126 homers, and 885 RBIs) and was elected to the Hall of Fame.

"He deserves it," Marion said. "He did a lot of work to get there. And he was a great shortstop . . . but I was better."

One time, early in my career, I fell behind in the count, 0–2. I had been striking out a lot, and I was afraid of piling up the strikeouts, so I choked up on the bat and tried to punch the ball to left field. The result was a weak ground ball to the shortstop.

When I got back to the dugout, Pee Wee called me over to sit next to him.

"What are you doing up there, giving up?" he said.

"What are you talking about?" I said.

"That wasn't your swing."

"I was just trying to punch the ball to left," I protested.

"Look," he said. "I'm the guy who's supposed to punch the ball and move it around because I bat at the top of the order. My job is to get on base any way I can. Your job is to drive me in."

Lesson learned.

Another thing Pee Wee was always getting on me for was fielding ground balls in the outfield. Ground balls were the weakest part of my game on defense, and I often went after them tentatively. When I did, Reese would be all over me.

"Come on, Duke," he would admonish. "Charge those balls. Be aggressive out there."

Those reminders helped me be more aggressive on ground balls, if only because I wanted to avoid the wrath of my captain.

That title, captain, was not one that Pee Wee took lightly. To him it was not just ceremonial. He took the role very seriously. There is no better evidence of his seriousness than how he interacted with Jackie Robinson.

Understand that, coming from Kentucky, Pee Wee's upbringing and culture were not much different from those players from the South who signed that petition against having Robinson as a teammate. But Pee Wee was a man of great decency, and he handled the situation exceptionally well, with dignity and humanity.

Pee Wee himself tells the story about his nervousness when the Dodgers signed Robinson. When Pee Wee heard about the Dodgers' black player in Montreal who was a shortstop, his eyes got as big as saucers and he said, "Uh-oh." Pee Wee said he was really glad when they put Jackie at first base.

A year later they moved Robinson from first base to second, and Reese and Robinson were not only teammates but also double play partners—a black man and a Southerner. It could have been a difficult situation, but through his actions and his class, Pee Wee made it easier. Even Jackie told people that Reese helped him more than any other player and that if it hadn't been for Pee Wee, he might not have been able to make it through those difficult early years.

Pee Wee did a lot of little things to show his support for Jackie, but nothing obvious. For instance, there were times I would be in center field when we were changing pitchers, and Pee Wee would wander over toward second base and I'd see him and Jackie talking. I never knew what they were talking about, but just the fact that they were talking had to ease the tension and anxiety for Jackie and make him feel like he belonged.

And then there was the famous incident when they were standing around second base and Pee Wee had his arm around Jackie. To be honest, I was there that day, but I don't remember seeing it happen. I must not have been looking their way or paying attention, but I heard about it, and I know it happened.

I can't say whether or not Pee Wee made the gesture consciously. Knowing him, I have to think he did. It was as if he was telling players on the other team, "When I look at this man, I don't see a black man; I see a man who is wearing a uniform that has the same team name on his shirt as I have on mine."

It doesn't show up in the numbers, but if everybody voting for the Hall of Fame knew how much [Pee Wee] meant to our ballclub, they wouldn't have waited so long to put him in.

Taking charge as a team leader, as the team captain, was only one of the ways Reese contributed to the Dodgers' success. There were other, more tangible ways. He played great defense, got on base, hit behind the runner, stole bases, and got big hits in the clutch. A lot of the things Reese did to help the Dodgers win you might not see in the box score.

I have always believed that Pee Wee would have made an excellent manager. I felt he had the right personality and temperament. He certainly had the baseball knowledge to be a successful manager.

There were rumors that he was offered the job in 1954 before they hired Walter Alston, but that he turned it down. I can't confirm any of those reports because we never talked about it, but I can believe both stories. If Reese did turn down the manager's job, it could have been for a few reasons. He probably felt he still had some good years left as a player, and he did, and he wouldn't have wanted the extra burden of being a player/manager.

I'm only guessing, but I also think he might not have wanted the responsibility. Every man knows himself, and Pee Wee probably knew he would take the losing too hard and that he would have a tough time cutting a player or being the disciplinarian a manager has to be. It just wasn't his nature.

The Veterans Committee finally elected Reese to the Hall of Fame in 1984, 26 years after he retired, 21 years after he was no longer eligible in the writers' vote. The reason it took so long is that Hall of Fame voting is largely a numbers game, and Pee Wee never had the kind of numbers that caught one's eye. He batted over .300 only once and had a career batting average of .269, he never hit more than 16 home runs in a season or drove in more than 84 runs, and he never stole more than 30 bases.

It doesn't show up in the numbers, but if everybody voting for the Hall of Fame knew how much he meant to our ballclub, they wouldn't have waited so long to put him in.

When it comes to being a team player and a leader, **Bill Russell** is the player I've seen that comes closest to Pee Wee Reese, and that's why I pick him as the number two all-time Dodgers shortstop, ahead of some guys whose numbers are more impressive.

Russell was a quiet leader who just went out and played solid baseball every day. He became more outspoken later in his career, but early on he led by example. Russell's value was in the things he did that aren't in the box score, although those weren't too bad, either—a career batting average of .263, 167 stolen bases, almost 800 runs scored, and steady, sometimes spectacular, defense.

Russell didn't play baseball in high school—his school did not have a baseball team. He was a basketball star, but the Dodgers signed him anyway because of his athleticism. Like Davey Lopes, Russell started out as a center

Bill Russell completes a double play during the 1981 World Series. *Photo courtesy of Focus on Sport/Getty Images.*

fielder. In his first three seasons with the Dodgers, he played only 7 games at short and 205 in the outfield.

At the time Walter Alston actually thought Russell would be a better center fielder than Willie Davis, but when Maury Wills looked like he was at the end of the line in 1972 and the Dodgers needed a shortstop to replace him, Alston moved Russell to the infield. In his first year there, when just learning to play the position, he led National League shortstops in errors. But Russell worked hard to improve and became one of the better shortstops in the league.

When he retired after the 1986 season, Russell had played more years (18) and in more games (2,181) as a Dodger than any other player, except Zack Wheat.

In the sixties, **Maury Wills** resurrected the stolen base, an art form that had been missing since the game's early days of Honus Wagner, Ty Cobb, and Max Carey. Wills led the National League in steals in each of his first six full seasons. In 1962 he broke Cobb's single-season stolen-base record with 104 and spawned a whole generation of base stealers, from Lou Brock to Rickey Henderson.

Wills was a remarkable success story, a role model for kids who may not be the best players on their Little League or high school teams. He was too small and too scrawny. Even after he signed a professional contract, he was never considered a prospect. He didn't have a position and wound up playing all over the lot before settling in at shortstop. He wasn't much of a hitter early in his career. In his first trial with the Dodgers, he had only seven RBIs in 83 games. In 1960, his first full season, he led National League shortstops in errors.

In the sixties, Maury Wills resurrected the stolen base, an art form that had been missing since the game's early days of Honus Wagner, Ty Cobb, and Max Carey. Wills led the National League in steals in each of his first six full seasons.

Like Bill Russell after him, Wills worked to improve his defense and used his speed and base-stealing ability as a weapon. He made himself into a good hitter and, as their leadoff man, was the catalyst that helped the Dodgers win four pennants in his eight years in Los Angeles.

Wills' breakout year came in 1962, when he not only broke Cobb's stolen-base record but also led the league with 10 triples; had career highs in runs scored (130), RBIs (48), home runs (6), at-bats (695, one below the major league record at the time), and hits (208); and was named Most Valuable Player in the National League.

Leo Durocher is best known as the controversial, flamboyant, hard-driving, win-at-all-costs, abrasive, umpire-baiting manager, and I'll talk about that Leo in the chapter on managers. As a player his reputation was that of a light-hitting but slick-fielding acrobatic shortstop, and—no surprise—a fiery competitor.

Durocher first got to the big leagues with the Yankees and played on their 1928 world championship team. He also developed his unsavory reputation early, with a story—never proven—that he stole Babe Ruth's watch, which may be the reason the Yankees sold him to Cincinnati.

Maury Wills steals his 96th base of the 1962 season in a game against the Cardinals. He got one more that day and later finished the season with 104.

Leo Durocher, known more for his managing days than his playing days, was a light-hitting, slick-fielding acrobatic shortstop.

Later he moved on to the Cardinals and was the shortstop and captain of the famed Gashouse Gang, the swashbuckling, hell-for-leather group that won the World Series in 1934; it was the perfect marriage of personalities between team and player.

After the 1937 season the Dodgers sent four players to the Cardinals in exchange for Durocher, who would play shortstop. Actually, he came over to the Dodgers as a manager-in-waiting. In 1939 he was a player/manager. The next season he turned his shortstop job over to Pee Wee Reese.

Leo ended his playing career after the 1945 season with a .247 lifetime batting average and only 24 home runs in 1,637 games. But his fame, his notoriety, and his legend were still ahead of him, as one of the most colorful and controversial managers the game has ever known.

Lonny Frey bats for the Cincinnati Reds against the Dodgers, his old club, during Johnny Vander Meer's second-consecutive no-hitter. *Photo courtesy of Bettmann/Corbis.*

I have only vague recollections of seeing **Lonny Frey** play, but I heard a lot about him from my older teammates, and what I heard was that he was an outstanding hitter—a left-handed hitting infielder (Editor's note: he switch-hit during his first six seasons). The glove I used in center field was a Lonny Frey model.

Frey's last season in the major leagues was my second. By that time he was at the end of his career.

Before Leo Durocher came to Brooklyn and took over the position, Frey was the Dodgers' shortstop for the first four years of his career. And he was a good one: an excellent fielder, a consistent .270 to .280 hitter, and a guy who could run.

Later Frey went to Cincinnati, which had an outstanding shortstop in Billy Myers, so Frey made the difficult switch to second base and became an even better second baseman than he was a shortstop. He made the All-Star team three times, led the league in steals in 1940, and helped the Reds win back-to-back pennants in 1939 and 1940.

Unfortunately, in the 1939 World Series against the Yankees, Frey was hitless in 17 at-bats, which stood as the record for World Series futility until my buddy and teammate Gil Hodges went hitless in 21 World Series at-bats 13 years later.

After his 0 for 17 in the 1939 World Series, Frey played in two more Series—two at-bats with the Reds in 1940 and one at-bat with the Yankees in 1947—and again was hitless. So he came to bat 20 times in three World Series and never got a hit.

It's one of the injustices of baseball: a guy has an outstanding 14-year major league career and it's all forgotten because of 20 World Series at-bats.

Statistical Summaries

All statistics are for player's Dodgers career only.

HITTING

G = Games

H = Hits

HR = Home runs

RBI = Runs batted in

SB = Stolen bases

BA = Batting average

Shortstop	Years	G	H	HR	RBI	SB	BA
Pee Wee Reese *Batted .345 with 10 hits in 1952 World Series*	1940–42 1946–58	2,166	2,170	126	885	232	.269
Bill Russell *Led NL with 25 intentional walks in 1974*	1969–86	2,181	1,926	46	627	167	.263
Maury Wills *Led NL in at-bats in both 1961 and 1962*	1959–66 1969–72	1,593	1,732	17	374	490	.281

continued	Years	G	H	HR	RBI	SB	BA
Leo Durocher *Made final out of Johnny Vander Meer's second no-hitter on June 15, 1938*	1938–41 1943, 1945	345	267	3	113	6	.244
Lonny Frey *Of his 125 hits in 1935, 57 went for extra bases*	1933–36	290	463	23	206	28	.278

FIELDING

PO = Putouts

A = Assists

E = Errors

DP = Double plays

TC/G = Total chances divided by games played

FA = Fielding average

Shortstop	PO	A	E	DP	TC/G	FA
Pee Wee Reese	4,040	5,891	388	1,246	5.1	.962
Bill Russell	2,536	5,546	339	909	4.8	.960
Maury Wills	2,464	4,630	272	822	4.9	.963
Leo Durocher	656	891	63	193	5.0	.961
Lonny Frey	800	1,183	148	216	5.5	.931

FIVE

Third Baseman

It's an unusual coincidence that three of the five third basemen on my list came to the Dodgers in trades on almost the same day, although in different years, and that all three of them had played other positions in Pittsburgh and became third basemen in Brooklyn.

Joseph Floyd "Arky" Vaughan got his nickname from his home state of Arkansas. He came to the Dodgers after 10 sensational years with the Pirates. In those 10 years he batted over .300 every season, including a league-leading .385 in 1935; made the All-Star team eight times; and was regarded as the number one shortstop in the game.

After the 1941 season, the Dodgers traded four players to get Vaughan and moved him to third base, a position Vaughan had never played regularly,

> 1. ARKY VAUGHAN
>
> 2. BILLY COX
>
> 3. RON CEY
>
> 4. COOKIE LAVAGETTO
>
> 5. JIM GILLIAM

but the Dodgers had Pee Wee Reese at short and needed to fill a hole at third. Arky fell to .277 in 1942, the first time he was below .300, but he bounced back to hit .305 in 1943.

After the 1943 season, Vaughan went home to his farm in Arkansas and refused to report for the 1944 season. It was believed that he stayed home to

69

support the war effort by farming, but the real reason may have been that he couldn't stand playing for Leo Durocher.

According to reports, Durocher had suspended pitcher Bobo Newsom for losing a game to the Pirates when he ignored a sign from catcher Bobby Bragan. Vaughan came to Newsom's defense and got into it with Durocher so vehemently that Arky, by all accounts a mild-mannered man, challenged Durocher to a fight.

The fight never happened, ruffled feathers were smoothed, and Vaughan finished out the 1943 season but refused to report the following year. Is it merely a coincidence that Vaughan returned to the Dodgers in 1947? True, World War II was over, but it's more significant that 1947 was the year Durocher served his suspension. After sitting out for three years, and at the age of 35, Vaughan batted .325 in 64 games as a part-time third baseman, out-fielder, and pinch-hitter. That's how good a hitter he was.

Brooklyn third baseman Arky Vaughan is tagged out at the plate by Cardinals pitcher Max Lanier after trying to score on a wild pitch during a September game in 1942.

It was in 1947, my rookie year, that I got to see Vaughan at the tail end of his career. A left-handed hitter, he was the nicest man, and I could see flashes of brilliance in him even though his career was almost over as a player.

Casey Stengel once said of Cox, "He ain't a third baseman, he's a blankety-blank acrobat," and that describes Billy to a T. He was an acrobat at third.

Vaughan finished his career with a lifetime batting average of .318, and he was elected posthumously to the Hall of Fame in 1985. Tragically, he drowned at the age of 40 in 1952, when he went fishing and the boat capsized.

Arky Vaughan's last year with the Dodgers, 1948, was **Billy Cox**'s first. Like Vaughan, Cox came from Pittsburgh, and like Vaughan, Billy was a shortstop for the Pirates. In one of the great trades in Dodgers history, the Dodgers sent three players to the Pirates for Cox, Preacher Roe, and Gene Mauch, who had been traded from the Dodgers to the Pirates just eight months before.

Among the three players the Dodgers sent to Pittsburgh was Dixie Walker, who had asked to be traded. The Dodgers were just as eager to deal Walker as he was to be dealt. He represented potential trouble because of his unwillingness to play on the same team as Jackie Robinson. Also, he was getting on in years, and the Dodgers wanted to move Carl Furillo from center to right and give me my shot at center. So, with one trade, the Dodgers not only got rid of a potential problem, but they also filled a void at third base, added a veteran starting pitcher, and opened up opportunities for two young players.

Cox's career got a late start because he spent four years in the military during World War II. After the war, he was the Pirates' starting shortstop for two seasons, 1946 and 1947, before being traded to the Dodgers. It wasn't until 1949 that he took over as the full-time third baseman—and what a third baseman he was.

Casey Stengel once said of Cox, "He ain't a third baseman, he's a blankety-blank acrobat," and that describes Billy to a T. He was an acrobat at third.

Cox was fun to watch. He had a little glove, not one of those basket gloves that third basemen wear today. He wasn't a big guy, only about 150 pounds, and he had slumped shoulders. He looked scrawny, but he could play. He had great, soft hands and he could pick it, and he had a strong, accurate arm. He'd throw the ball to first base about four feet high so that sometimes the pitcher would have to duck out of the way. I don't remember him ever making a bad throw to first. He must have, but I don't remember it.

Billy also had this habit on hard-hit balls: he'd flick that little glove like a serpent's tongue and snatch the hot shot. Then he'd hold the ball and look at it, as if he were counting the stitches, and then he'd gun the ball to first base and just nip the runner by half a step.

Cox wasn't a great hitter, a lifetime .262 batter, but occasionally he would show surprising power. He was a high-ball hitter, and every once in a while he'd pop the ball into the left-field stands in Ebbets Field.

Billy and I got to be good friends after we became teammates, but it didn't start out that way. When he was with the Pirates, he got a hit to center field one day and tried to stretch it into a double. I threw to second base, and the ball hit him on the head. They had to carry him off the field.

Cox roomed with Preacher Roe, who also came from the Pirates, and what a couple of characters they were. They both liked to play poker. One night they were playing, and one hand seemed to go on forever. The table was covered with dollar bills, and Billy was running out of money. But he didn't want to drop out because he had a good hand, so he wrote a check for $200 to cover his bet.

Billy won the hand, and the first thing he did was pick up his check and tear it into little pieces. "It's a good thing I won that hand," he said. "If my wife had seen a canceled check for that much money, she would have killed me."

During the time he was with the Dodgers, from 1948 to 1954, Cox was generally regarded as the best-fielding third baseman in the game. I never saw a third baseman field better than Billy Cox did. I saw third basemen hit better, but not field better. In fact, he was considered the best-fielding third baseman ever until Brooks Robinson came along. I didn't see much of Robinson, except in the World Series, and he was great, but I can't imagine him being any better than Cox was.

Coincidentally, Cox was traded to Baltimore after the 1954 season, and he played in 53 games for the Orioles in 1955, the year Brooks Robinson first got to Baltimore.

After Billy Cox left the Dodgers, third base was handled by a cast of what seemed like thousands—everyone from Jackie Robinson, Jim Gilliam, Randy Jackson, Ken McMullen, John Kennedy, and Jim Lefebvre to Bob Bailey, Bill Sudakis, and Billy Grabarkewitz. Even Pee Wee Reese and Steve Garvey had a shot there.

Billy Cox (second from right) was best known for his acrobatic defensive plays at third base. Others pictured (from left) are Jackie Robinson, Gil Hodges, Roy Campanella, and Pee Wee Reese.

And then in 1973 along came **Ron Cey**, "the Penguin," and the Dodgers' third base problem was solved for 10 years.

They called him "the Penguin" because he was built close to the ground, short and stocky, with short, stumpy legs and a choppy running style. As so often happens in baseball, somebody watched Cey run and remarked that he ran like a penguin, so, naturally, the nickname stuck.

Despite his size, Cey was a powerful hitter and a hard-nosed player. He hit 20 or more home runs for the Dodgers for six straight years and would have made it seven straight except for the players strike in 1981. He came back the next year to hit 24 home runs, and then he was traded to the Cubs and hit 20 or more home runs for them three years in a row.

In all, Cey hit 316 home runs in a 17-year career. He also drove in 1,139 runs and had a lifetime batting average of .261.

Ron Cey (right) gets congratulations from teammates Dusty Baker (left) and Davey Lopes after his three-run home run clinched a World Series game against the Yankees in 1978.

There had to be times when he watched Ron Cey, or tracked his career, that Ron Santo thought he was looking at his clone 15 years later, so strikingly similar were the careers of the two Rons.

Both were born in the state of Washington in the month of February—Santo in Seattle, Cey in Tacoma—eight years and 10 days apart. Both were outstanding National League All-Star third basemen. Both were strong, right-handed hitters and big run-producers for their respective teams. And they had similar builds—Santo, 6', 190 pounds, and Cey, 5'10', 185 pounds.

"When Ron came up to the big leagues with the Dodgers and I met him," said Santo, "he told me he kind of followed in my footsteps, and if you look at his numbers, you'll see how close we were."

The closeness, indeed, is eerie:

Santo: four seasons with 100 or more RBIs, 11 seasons with 20 or more home runs, nine times a member of the National League All-Star team.

Cey: two seasons with 100 or more RBIs, nine seasons with 20 or more home runs, six times a member of the National League All-Star team.

Santo: 2,243 games, 8,143 at-bats, 2,254 hits, 1,138 runs, 342 home runs, 1,331 RBIs, and a career .277 batting average.

Cey: 2,073 games, 7,162 at-bats, 1,868 hits, 977 runs, 316 home runs, 1,139 RBIs, and a career .261 batting average.

When Cey arrived in the big leagues in 1971, Santo was an established star, one of the premier third basemen in the game. In 1973, Cey's first full major league season, Santo was the National League's starting third baseman in the All-Star Game. A year later, as Santo was playing his final season as a member of the Chicago White Sox, Cey was the National League's starting third baseman in the All-Star Game.

"Cey was a great ballplayer," Santo said. "Good hitter, good fielder, and a guy who always played the game hard. I had a lot of respect for him as a player."

To keep the comparison with Santo going, Cey was traded to the Cubs in 1983, nine years after Santo played his last game.

"I was retired," Santo said, "but Chicago was my home and I saw a lot of Cubs games, so I saw Ron play a lot of games in my old position."

In 1984, his second season as a Cub, Cey led the team in home runs with 25. That was the most home runs by a Cubs third baseman since 1965, when the Cubs third baseman belted 33. His name was Ron Santo.

Harry "Cookie" Lavagetto is one of the great names, and one of the great heroes, in Brooklyn baseball. He's also one of the great people in the game it was my pleasure to know. Lavagetto's last year with the Dodgers was 1947, my rookie year. But I got to know him better later when he was a coach with the Dodgers from 1951 through 1953, and again in 1963 when I joined the New York Mets, where Cookie was a coach under Casey Stengel.

Lavagetto is the third Dodgers third baseman to come from Pittsburgh. He came to Brooklyn after the 1936 season. He had played mostly second base for the Pirates and split his time between second and third in his first year with the Dodgers, before taking over as their third baseman in 1938.

Lavagetto played for the Dodgers from 1937 to 1947, with four years off for military service in World War II. He had his best year in 1939, with career highs in batting average (.300), home runs (10), and RBIs (87), but his career is defined by one pinch-hit against the Yankees in the 1947 World Series. It not only was one of the great moments in Brooklyn Dodgers history, but it was also one of the great moments in World Series history.

Cookie was 35 years old at the time and at the end of his career. He had played in only 41 games for the Dodgers that season and was used mostly as a pinch-hitter. He happened to be in the right place at the right time in Ebbets Field on the afternoon of October 3, 1947, Game 4 of the World Series.

I had played in only 40 games for the Dodgers in my rookie season, so I was not included on their World Series roster. I stayed to watch the first two games of the Series because I had never been to Yankee Stadium. But Bev and I were getting married that fall, so I went home to California after the second game and listened to the rest of the World Series the way I did when I was a kid, on the radio. So I never got to see the famous catch Dodgers left fielder Al Gionfriddo made against Joe DiMaggio in Game 6 (I later heard from my teammates that the reason it was such a great catch was that Gionfriddo misjudged the ball and had to run down his mistake), and I never got to see Lavagetto's big hit.

The Yankees won the first two games, but the Dodgers came back to win Game 3 at home. In the fourth game they faced Bill Bevens, a journeyman right-hander who had won only seven games and lost thirteen during the regular season. But on that afternoon, Bevens was pitching the game of his life.

Going into the ninth inning, the Yankees led, 2–1, and Bevens was pitching a no-hitter (the Dodgers had scored their run in the fifth on two walks, a sacrifice, and a fielder's choice).

Up to that time there had never been a no-hitter pitched in the World Series (Don Larsen's perfect game would come nine years later), and Bevens

Cookie Lavagetto (right) shares a laugh with Hugh Casey at Ebbets Field during the 1947 World Series. *Photo courtesy of Bettmann/Corbis.*

was two outs away when he got Bruce Edwards to fly to center. Bevens then walked Carl Furillo, his ninth walk of the game, but Spider Jorgensen fouled out, and Bevens was then one out away from a no-hitter.

Al Gionfriddo was sent in to run for Furillo, and Pete Reiser batted for Hugh Casey. With Reiser at bat, Gionfriddo stole second, leaving first base open. At that point, Yankees manager Bucky Harris took a gamble and ordered Reiser intentionally walked. Harris' decision went against the book that says you don't put the winning run on base.

Eddie Miksis was then sent in to run for Reiser, who had a bad ankle, and Dodgers manager Burt Shotton sent Lavagetto up to hit for Eddie Stanky.

It was a curious and daring move. Lavagetto, a part-time player, had only 18 hits all season. Stanky, a regular, had 141 hits and was known as a tough hitter in the clutch, a guy who could always find a way to beat you.

Why Lavagetto instead of Stanky?

Call it fate.

Lavagetto sent a high, lazy fly ball toward the right-field fence. The ball hit off the fence, and with the runners off at the crack of the bat, Gionfriddo scored from second and Miksis was right behind him, scoring the winning run from first. Gone was Bevens' no-hitter. The Dodgers won, 3–2, and Cookie Lavagetto was a Brooklyn hero for the ages.

As an ironic footnote to history, after the World Series was over, with the Yankees winning in seven games, Lavagetto, Bevens, and Gionfriddo—the principals in one of the most memorable World Series games ever played—never played another major league game.

I talked about **Jim Gilliam** in the chapter on second basemen, about what an outstanding offensive player he was and how, when he arrived, the Dodgers shifted Jackie Robinson from second base to third. Now, I'll tell you about Gilliam as number five on my list of all-time Dodgers third basemen.

When Robinson could no longer play second base at a high level because of his bad knees, he moved to left field and then to third base. And Gilliam did exactly the same thing.

The Dodgers had come up with a terrific young player named Charlie Neal, who looked like he was going to be the guy to replace Pee Wee Reese at shortstop. Charlie was erratic at short, but the Dodgers wanted to get his bat in the lineup, so when the team moved to Los Angeles in 1958, they put Neal at second and moved Gilliam to left field.

Like Robinson had before him, Jim Gilliam (left) moved from second base to third base and gave the Dodgers eight seasons of stability at that position. *Photo courtesy of Time & Life Pictures/Getty Images.*

Third base continued to be a trouble spot, and the following year, Gilliam was brought in to play third base, again taking the same path Robinson had taken before him.

For the next eight years, Gilliam gave the Dodgers some stability at third base, although the ever-versatile Gilliam occasionally was called on to plug other holes at second and in the outfield. All the while, Gilliam continued to produce offensively, getting hits, drawing walks, stealing bases, and scoring runs, and he played a solid third base on four pennant winners and three World Series champions.

Statistical Summaries

All statistics are for player's Dodgers career only.

HITTING

G = Games
H = Hits
HR = Home runs
RBI = Runs batted in
SB = Stolen bases
BA = Batting average

Third Baseman	Years	G	H	HR	RBI	SB	BA
Arky Vaughan *Struck out only 13 times in 610 at-bats in 1943*	1942–43 1947–48	406	394	12	162	32	.291
Billy Cox *Hit three doubles and a home run and had six RBIs in the 1953 World Series*	1948–54	742	659	46	245	31	.259
Ron Cey *Drove in eight against the Padres on July 31, 1974*	1971–82	1,481	1,378	228	842	20	.264

continued	Years	G	H	HR	RBI	SB	BA
Cookie Lavagetto *Had six hits in six at-bats against the Phillies on September 23, 1939*	1937–41, 1946–47	818	763	35	395	56	.275
Jim Gilliam *Ranked in top five base stealers in NL each year from 1955 to 1959*	1953–66	1,956	1,889	65	558	203	.265

FIELDING

PO = Putouts

A = Assists

E = Errors

DP = Double plays

TC/G = Total chances divided by games played

FA = Fielding average

Third Baseman	PO	A	E	DP	TC/G	FA
Arky Vaughan	187	322	18	24	2.7	.966
Billy Cox	640	1,206	68	149	2.9	.964
Ron Cey	1,196	3,124	166	252	3.1	.963
Cookie Lavagetto	695	1,124	120	105	3.0	.938
Jim Gilliam	533	1,265	90	110	2.5	.952

SIX

Left Fielder

Joe "Ducky" Medwick is another of my childhood idols and another player I heard a lot about from Pee Wee Reese. Before coming to the Dodgers, Medwick was a star with the Cardinals' Gashouse Gang. He was a notorious bad-ball hitter, but he was a great hitter who never batted lower than .300 in his eight years in St. Louis, had three straight years with more than 200 hits, and is the last National Leaguer to win the Triple Crown— 31 home runs, 154 RBIs, and a .374 batting average in 1937.

A lifetime .324 hitter and a terrific run-producer who led the league in RBIs three straight years in the midthirties, Medwick is in the Hall of Fame but is probably best remembered for a controversial incident in Detroit in the seventh game of the 1934 World Series between the Cardinals and the Tigers.

In the sixth inning Medwick hit one off the right-center-field bleachers to drive in Pepper Martin and put the Cardinals ahead 8–0. In his typical all-out fashion, Medwick raced around the bases and slid hard into third base,

1. JOE MEDWICK

2. TOMMY DAVIS

3. ZACK WHEAT

4. AUGIE GALAN

5. LOU JOHNSON

Joe Medwick, a Hall of Famer, spent only three seasons with the Dodgers but was the missing piece to the puzzle in 1941 when Brooklyn won its first pennant in 21 years.

upending Tigers third baseman Marv Owen, who still hadn't received the throw from the outfield.

The Tigers fans were enraged. When Medwick went out to play left field in the bottom of the inning, the fans pelted left field with bottles, food, and all kinds of garbage. Commissioner Kenesaw Mountain Landis who was at the game, ordered the umpires to remove Medwick from the game "for his own protection." Medwick left the field to a chorus of boos, and the Cardinals won the game, 11–0, and the World Series.

In June 1940, the Dodgers got Medwick and Curt Davis from the Cardinals for four players and a staggering sum for that time—$125,000. It was another great deal pulled off by Larry MacPhail and one that manager Leo Durocher enthusiastically endorsed. Durocher was getting a comrade-in-arms and the kind of rough-and-tumble player he prized. He and Medwick had been teammates and friends when both were part of the Cardinals' Gashouse Gang.

Medwick had slipped, but he was only three years removed from his Triple Crown season, and he still had a lot of good baseball left in him. Unfortunately, in his first game as a Dodger—which was against his former team, the Cardinals—Medwick was hit on the head by a pitch. Still, he came back to bat .300, hit 14 home runs, and drive in 66 runs in 106 games to help the Dodgers move up from third place in 1939 to second in 1940.

Medwick was a Dodger for only three seasons and parts of two others, but he made a major impact in Brooklyn. He was the missing piece to the puzzle in 1941, batting .318 with 18 home runs and 88 RBIs to help the Dodgers win their first pennant in 21 years.

Medwick was sold to the Giants midway through the 1943 season, went on to the Boston Braves, and then went back to the Dodgers in 1946. He left Brooklyn after the 1946 season, the year before I arrived, and finished out his career as a part-time player with the Cardinals. I must have seen him play, but I have no recollection of it. I did meet him later on, however.

I was managing Albuquerque, the Dodgers' Double A farm team in the Texas League, and Joe was a minor league hitting instructor for the Cardinals. We went into Little Rock, Arkansas, early in the season, and Medwick was there. We were talking, and he said, kind of sarcastically, "Hey, you got a bunch of expensive young kids on that ballclub. You think you're going to do all right?"

I said, "If we can stay close for a couple of months, Joe, we'll win the league."

"Really!"

"Yeah," I said.

It was obvious Medwick didn't think much of our team.

A couple months later, we went back to Little Rock, and we were in first place by a game or two. I saw Medwick again, and he asked me how we were in first place with these young kids.

"Joe," I said, "the kids developed."

The next day in the paper, Medwick was quoted as saying, "Snider's got a Triple A ballclub over there."

This was the same guy who didn't think we had a chance to win the pennant when he first saw us a few months earlier.

I've been around this game a long time, almost 60 years, and I've never seen a hitter have a better year than **Tommy Davis** did in 1962, my last year with the Dodgers. He should have been the Most Valuable Player. He finished third in the voting, behind Maury Wills and Willie Mays.

I don't mean to take anything away from Wills. That was the year he broke Ty Cobb's stolen-base record with 104 and was the catalyst for the Dodgers' offense. He batted .299 and scored 130 runs, but in most of the 130 runs Wills scored, he was driven in by Tommy Davis, and I have always believed that the guy who knocks in runs is more valuable than the guy who scores them.

Tommy led the National League with 153 runs batted in. He led the league with 230 hits. And he led the league with a .346 batting average. He also hit 27 home runs, the most he ever hit in a season. But Davis wasn't a home-run hitter, and that's what kept him from winning the Triple Crown. Mays hit 49 that year.

But if you're talking about big hits, clutch hits, and if you're talking about line drives, you should be talking about Tommy Davis in 1962. He got so many big hits. He hit so many line drives. And he could run—that was before he broke his ankle. He had 27 doubles and nine triples that season, and he stole 18 bases.

He followed up that season with his second consecutive batting championship in 1963, when he batted .326 and was the first National Leaguer to win back-to-back batting titles since Stan Musial did it 11 years earlier. Two years later he broke his ankle and never was the same player again, but he

Tommy Davis was not able to keep this ball from leaving the field at Dodger Stadium during the 1966 World Series against the Baltimore Orioles. *Photo courtesy of Focus on Sport/Getty Images.*

never lost his ability to hit. He became a traveling man, playing for nine different teams in 10 years, and found a home in Baltimore as a designated hitter, and later as a superb pinch-hitter.

Tommy was born and raised in Brooklyn and was a standout basketball player in high school and a teammate of NBA legend Lenny Wilkens. He had many offers to play college basketball, but he chose baseball and signed with the Dodgers, thanks in large part to the urging of his idol, Jackie Robinson.

By the time Davis reached the major leagues in 1959, the Dodgers had left Brooklyn, so he never got to play for his hometown team (although he did spend a year with the Mets), but he did make his mark in Los Angeles, and elsewhere.

ene Tenace was a young player with the Oakland Athletics trying to make his bones as a major leaguer—still a couple of years away from his big, breakout 1972 World Series—when he first met Tommy Davis. (In the 1972 World Series, Tenace became the first player in history to hit home runs in his first two Series at-bats, belted two more homers, drove in nine runs, batted .348, and was named Series MVP.)

The year was 1970, and Davis' contract had been purchased by the Athletics from the Houston Astros. He would stay with Oakland until September, when he was sold to the Chicago Cubs, and then Davis would return to Oakland the following season, signing as a free agent.

By then Davis was a 10-year veteran, past his prime and eight years beyond his two consecutive National League batting championships. Although he was only 32 years old, a broken ankle he suffered six years earlier had slowed him down, and the A's were his seventh team in five years. He would never again be the same player he had been with the Dodgers in the early sixties, a young slugger with Hall of Fame potential.

"He couldn't run as well as he used to, but he could still hit," said Tenace. "Could he hit! He was a great hitter. And what a great guy."

Davis appeared in 79 games for Oakland in 1971, batted a robust .324, drove in 42 runs, and struck out only 19 times in 219 at-bats.

Here, Tenance shares his thoughts on Davis:

[Editor's note: The rule allowing designated hitters came into effect in 1973.] He was mostly a designated hitter [although he appeared in 35 games at first base, 16 in the outfield, 3 at second base, and 2 at third]. I learned a lot just watching him hit and talking to him. One day he said to me, "You gotta slap the midget." I said, "Tommy, what are you talking about?"

He said, "Visualize there's a little guy standing right there"—and he pointed to a spot a few inches in front of him and about three feet off the ground—"and then you just hit him with the back of your hand.

That's the way you want to swing the bat. You have to slap the midget." He used to say that all the time, *"Slap the midget."*

Tommy could hit the ball to the opposite field as well as any right-handed hitter I ever played with. He'd talk about letting the ball travel, meaning letting it get in on him, and then swinging down on the ball. I was always fascinated being around him and just watching how he went about his business, how serious he took hitting.

He was a natural hitter. What impressed me was how he could hit the ball to the opposite field and always on a line. I rarely saw him hit a lazy fly ball to right field; it was always a line drive. He didn't hit a lot of home runs, and Tommy's a big guy [6'2", 195 pounds in his playing days]. But it seemed like he was more concerned about just hitting the ball hard somewhere instead of hitting the ball over the fence. I think if he made up his mind to wait for a pitch and zone in on a pitch, he could hit the ball out of the ballpark. There's no doubt in my mind that if he made his mind up to hit the ball out of the ball-park, he could hit it out of the ballpark—that's how good a hitter he was. Most of the time he just hit the ball where it was pitched.

He had great patience at the plate, great discipline, and a great swing—a short, compact swing. For a guy his size, his stride was so short, and his swing was so short, and he stayed on top of the ball. His mind-set wasn't to go up there and hit a home run. He would try to get a good pitch to hit and hit it hard someplace. That's what made him such a great hitter.

If you want to compare him to a hitter of recent times, I'd say he was a lot like Edgar Martinez, who also had a short, compact swing and hit the ball to all fields like Tommy did. They both had great gap power.

Tommy was one of the true professionals I had the opportunity to play with, and one of the best teammates I ever had. What a class act he was. His personality and disposition was one of the best of all the guys I ever played with. He was unbelievable. He always had a smile on his face.

One thing I remember about him is that he loved sweets. On Sundays, somebody would bring in a bunch of doughnuts and

Tommy would go right to the table where the doughnuts were, and he'd eat these powdered doughnuts and wind up with powder all over his face.

But what a great guy. I really enjoyed being around him. The last time I saw Tommy was at Joe Rudi's charity golf tournament in Modesto, California. I hadn't seen him for several years, and he was the same Tommy. He came up to me and gave me a hug. He looked great, and he had the same personality—always smiling.

Because he could hit, Tommy was always able to get a job. He wound up playing for 10 different major league teams. He split 1976, his final big-league season, between the California Angels and Kansas City Royals, and, at the age of 37, hardly able to run, he batted .381 as a pinch-hitter. When he retired, Tommy had a career batting average of .294, and his career pinch-hitting average was .320, the highest in baseball history.

As good a career as he had, you have to wonder how much better it would have been if he had been able to stay healthy. There's an old saying in baseball that applies perfectly to Tommy Davis: "Wake him up in a snowstorm at 4:00 on Christmas morning, and he'll hit a line drive."

It's impossible to be a Brooklyn Dodger, or even a fan of Brooklyn baseball, and not be familiar with the name **Zack Wheat**. One reason is the name itself: so colorful, so unique, so unforgettable. Another, more important, reason is what this man accomplished: a lifetime batting average of .317 for 19 major league seasons, all but one of them in Brooklyn, and he was elected to the Hall of Fame in 1959. Almost 80 years after he played his last game, Wheat still is on the top of the Dodgers all-time lists for games (2,322), at-bats (8,859), hits (2,804), doubles (464), triples (171), and total bases (4,003).

He wasn't a big man, only 5'10", 170 pounds, and he wasn't a home-run hitter (playing mostly in baseball's dead-ball era, he hit only 132 homers in 19 seasons), but he was one of Brooklyn's first superstars, its second batting champion, and the team's cleanup hitter for most of his career. And he was amazingly consistent, a great left-handed contact hitter who batted over .300 in 13 of his 19 years and never struck out more than 52 times in any

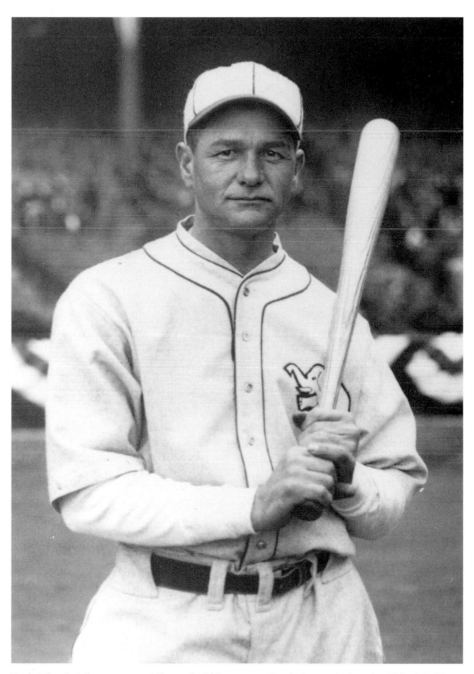

Zack Wheat strikes a pose at the end of his career, after being traded to the Philadelphia Athletics following a long and brilliant career in Brooklyn.

Augie Galan (top row, second from right) poses with the 1941 National League champion
Brooklyn Dodgers.

one season except his first, in which he struck out 80 times. So adept was Wheat at hitting the curveball that there are stories that Giants manager John McGraw threatened to fine any of his pitchers who threw Wheat a curve. Oh, how I wish managers had done the same thing with me!

Playing in an era of colorful players and with a team noted for its crazy antics, Wheat had the reputation of being a gentleman and a quiet leader. How much of a gentleman, and how quiet? In 2,410 games, he never was thrown out of a game. Not once.

[Augie Galan] was the first regular player ever to play an entire season and not hit into a double play. In 1935 he came to bat 646 times and didn't hit into one double play—but he did hit into a triple play.

Augie Galan is another guy I just missed with the Dodgers. Like Joe Medwick, his last season in Brooklyn was 1946, the year before I got there. He moved on to Cincinnati and then to the Giants, and I got to see him play, but by then he was at the end of his career.

Earlier, he had been an outstanding player for the Cubs, batting over .300 twice, leading the National League in runs scored once and in stolen bases twice. The Dodgers acquired him to help them in their stretch run to the 1941 pennant, and he gave them five more good years, hitting over .300 three times, twice leading the league in walks, and twice driving in more than 90 runs.

When I saw him, Galan was a left-handed hitter, but earlier in his career, he was a switch-hitter, and in 1937 he became the first player in National League history to hit home runs from both sides of the plate in one game.

Here's another interesting fact about Galan: he was the first regular player ever to play an entire season and not hit into a double play. In 1935 he came to bat 646 times and didn't hit into one double play—but he did hit into one triple play.

There are several players I could pick as number five among Dodgers left fielders and not go wrong with the choice. There's Luis Olmo, Andy Pafko, Dusty Baker, Gary Sheffield, Wally Moon, even Jackie Robinson and Jim Gilliam. But I'm partial to **Lou Johnson**.

I managed "Sweet Lou" in Spokane, Washington, in 1965. He had had trials with the Cubs, Angels, and Braves, and he had a reputation, undeserved, of being a hard guy to handle. I found him to be a joy to manage. Lou and I

Lou Johnson reacts to being called out at second base during the 1965 World Series against the Minnesota Twins. *Photo courtesy of Focus on Sport/Getty Images.*

94

became very good friends. Whenever I see him, he comes over to me and says, "Thanks for sending me up."

Early in the 1965 season, Tommy Davis broke his ankle and I got a call from Buzzie Bavasi.

"We need an outfielder; who have you got?"

"I only have one guy," I said. "Lou Johnson."

"Lou Johnson?" he said. "He's been in the big leagues a few times."

I said, "Buzzie, you put this guy in the lineup and leave him alone. If you don't play him, if he has a bad night and Alston takes him out of the lineup, it'll kill him. Let him play. Let him relax, and let him play."

Lou went up and had a few very good years. He helped the Dodgers win the pennant in 1965 and 1966. You had to admire a guy like Lou Johnson. He spent 10 years in the minor leagues before he got his chance in the big leagues, and then he made the most of it.

He never put up gaudy numbers with the Dodgers, just a .259 average, 12 home runs, and 58 RBIs in 1965 and a .272 average, 17 homers, and 73 RBIs in 1966, but what those numbers don't tell you is how many clutch hits he got, how many games he helped the Dodgers win, and the little things he did on the field and in the clubhouse that contributed to two championships.

Statistical Summaries

All statistics are for player's Dodgers career only.

HITTING

G = Games

H = Hits

HR = Home runs

RBI = Runs batted in

SB = Stolen bases

BA = Batting average

Left Fielder	Years	G	H	HR	RBI	SB	BA
Joe Medwick *Had two hits and a run scored in Game 2 of the 1941 World Series*	1941–43 1946	470	535	38	293	7	.303
Tommy Davis *Batting champ in 1962 and 1963; first NL player to repeat since Stan Musial (1950 and 1952)*	1959–66	821	912	86	465	65	.304

continued	Years	G	H	HR	RBI	SB	BA
Zack Wheat *Had three hitting streaks of 24 games or longer (29, 26, 24)*	1909–26	2,322	2,804	131	1,210	203	.317
Augie Galan *Collected hits in eight consecutive at-bats during 1944 season*	1941–46	627	640	33	316	33	.301
Lou Johnson *Led NL in being hit by pitches, with 14 in 1966*	1965–67	387	353	40	172	27	.267

FIELDING

PO = Putouts

A = Assists

E = Errors

DP = Double plays

TC/G = Total chances divided by games played

FA = Fielding average

Left Fielder	PO	A	E	DP	TC/G	FA
Joe Medwick	892	25	15	3	2.1	.984
Tommy Davis	1,098	41	32	10	1.7	.973
Zack Wheat	4,891	224	181	53	2.3	.966
Augie Galan	985	32	21	6	2.4	.980
Lou Johnson	601	18	11	4	1.7	.983

SEVEN

Center Fielder

I have already mentioned that one of the reasons I became a Dodgers fan was Pete Reiser. I was 14 years old in 1941 and beginning to get really interested in baseball. I'd get *The Sporting News* and read about the Dodgers, who won the pennant that year, and about Reiser, who was stealing home and doing all kinds of exciting things. Little did I realize that just six years later I would be Reiser's teammate, and two years after that I would take his place as the Dodgers' center fielder.

Actually, when I first came to the Dodgers in 1947, Reiser was playing left field. He had been slowed by a series of injuries and could no longer run like he used to, so Burt Shotton moved him to left and put Carl Furillo at center. It was Shotton who eventually moved Furillo to right field and gave me the center-field job.

1. PETE REISER

2. WILLIE DAVIS

3. BRETT BUTLER

4. RICK MONDAY

5. MAX CAREY

Many years later, in another ironic twist, I replaced Reiser again. Pete was managing in the Dodgers' farm system at Spokane, Washington, when he suffered a heart attack. The Dodgers asked me to take over the team in his place, which I did.

97

Pete Reiser won the 1941 batting title at age 22, the youngest National League player ever to do so.

98

Although I got to see Reiser play, I didn't see a lot of him and I didn't see him at his best. By the time I was a regular, in 1949, Pete had been traded to the Boston Braves. But I heard a lot about Reiser from Pee Wee Reese. They had come up to the Dodgers together in 1940, were only eight months apart in age, had the same first name (Harold), and were close friends. In fact, they seemed to be inseparable when people talked about the Dodgers. Reese and Reiser. You hardly ever heard one name without the other.

What Mickey Mantle was, Pete Reiser—a player with enormous power and such blazing speed that they called him "Pistol Pete"—could have been. Like Mantle, Reiser could hit from both sides of the plate, although he batted strictly left-handed early in his career and didn't switch-hit until the latter part of his career. Pee Wee said that Reiser was the most exciting player he'd ever seen, and that includes Jackie Robinson, so that's pretty exciting.

In his first full season, 1941, Reiser led the National League in doubles with 39, triples with 17, runs scored with 117, slugging percentage with .558, and batting average with .343. At the age of 22, he was the youngest man to win the National League batting championship. He finished second in the Most Valuable Player voting to his teammate Dolph Camilli, who led the league in home runs and RBIs. But you could make a case that Reiser deserved the award. His potential seemed unlimited.

"[Reiser] might have been the best ballplayer I ever saw. He had everything but luck."

—LEO DUROCHER

Tommy Holmes, who won a batting title with the Braves, once said Reiser was "as great a star as there ever was in the game." And Leo Durocher, who played with Babe Ruth and managed Willie Mays, said, "[Reiser] might have been the best ballplayer I ever saw. He had everything but luck."

You can say that Reiser's bad luck was self-inflicted. He was a fearless and reckless outfielder who would let nothing stop him from catching the ball, and that proved to be his undoing. On July 19, 1942, Reiser was batting .379 when he smashed into the center-field wall in St. Louis. He suffered a severe concussion and a separated shoulder (there were no warning tracks or padding on the outfield walls in those days). Reiser missed more than a month of the season, and his batting average dropped to .310.

Reiser's three years of military service also contributed to the erosion of his skills. When he returned in 1946, he wasn't the same player he had been. He batted only .277, but he did lead the league in stolen bases and set a major league record by stealing home seven times.

And he kept crashing into walls.

One writer said that Reiser was carried off the field 11 times in his career. In 1947 he crashed into the center-field wall in Ebbets Field and was hurt so badly that he was given last rites.

From that point on, Reiser's career just spiraled downward. But one positive thing did come out of Reiser's injuries. His frequent mishaps from crashing into walls prompted teams to pad the outfield walls and to install warning tracks in the outfield. People speculate that he also may have been the reason for the batting helmet. It started when players had plastic bands sewn into their caps to protect their heads from wild pitches. Those bands were the forerunner to batting helmets, which are mandatory for all batters today.

99

All those innovations came about too late to save Reiser's career. By many accounts, he was the greatest baseball talent Brooklyn has ever seen, and he undoubtedly would have ended up in the Hall of Fame if only he could have avoided slamming into outfield walls.

Willie Davis didn't play high school baseball, but the Dodgers signed him anyway because he had great natural athletic ability. They turned him over to Kenny Myers, who was a scout and a hitting instructor for the Dodgers.

Willie Davis, never having played baseball in high school, turned himself into a great player who enjoyed an 18-year major league career.

Myers took Davis and started from scratch. He taught Davis how to throw the ball, how to catch the ball, how to field the ball, and how to hit. And if Willie Davis had taken care of himself the way he needed to, he could have been a Hall of Famer. He had that kind of potential. He was a self-made player with outstanding ability.

Willie had blinding speed. It wasn't so evident when he went from home to first, but once he got in gear, going from home to third or from first to third, he was the fastest player in the game. It was when he rounded the first base in his path that he picked up speed with those long strides. He probably could have been an Olympic sprinter, or a quarter-miler. He didn't think anybody could run with him. Defensively, he thought he could outrun the ball.

Willie had blinding speed. It wasn't so evident when he went from home to first, but once he got in gear, going from home to third or from first to third, he was the fastest player in the game.

Davis made himself into a good player. He was the Dodgers' center fielder for 13 seasons, from 1961 to 1973, and he won three Gold Gloves. He consistently batted in the .280 to .290 range, with three seasons over .300, and he stole more than 20 bases for 11 consecutive seasons, with a high of 42 in 1964. Willie spent 18 years in the major leagues and had a fine career, but he could have been so much better.

For all the great things he accomplished, it's unfortunate that Davis is probably always going to be remembered for one game . . . no, one inning—the fifth—in Game 2 of the 1966 World Series against the Orioles. Willie lost two balls in the sun and was charged with three errors in the inning. The Orioles broke a scoreless tie with three runs in the inning, went on to beat the Dodgers 6–0, and then won the next two games at home to complete a four-game sweep.

Brett Butler came to the Dodgers in 1991 after 10 outstanding seasons with the Braves, Indians, and Giants and was the Dodgers' center fielder and lead-off hitter for the next four years, averaging .296, .309, .298, and .314 and stealing 38, 41, 39, and 27 bases over those four years. Butler was a great leadoff man who knew his capabilities and knew why he was in the lineup—to lead off and get on base—and he did it exceptionally well. He did all the little things: run, bunt, steal, and draw a walk, and he played a good center field. He didn't have a great arm, but he charged the ball well. And he was very competitive. When the umpire said, "Play ball," he played ball.

Brett Butler connects for a triple to drive in two runs against the Colorado Rockies at Coors Field on September 28, 1997.

After leaving the Dodgers as a free agent in 1995, Butler came back later that season and was a part-time player who batted .274, .267, and .283 and stole 39 bases in 178 games over three years. In his final season, at age 40, he batted .283 and stole 15 bases in 105 games.

In his career, Butler batted over .300 six times, had more than 90 walks five times, scored more than 100 runs six times, stole more than 40 bases five times, had an on-base percentage over .400 three times, was considered one of the best bunters in the game, and played sure-handed and wide-ranging defense in center field.

In 1976 in a game at Dodger Stadium, **Rick Monday** gained national attention and became a hero to many Americans. Playing center field for the Cubs at the time, Monday noticed that two men had jumped onto the field carrying an American flag and appeared to be preparing to set the flag on fire. Rick ran after the guys. One of them threw a can of lighter fluid at Monday, just missing him. Rick continued the chase and grabbed the flag out of their hands before they could desecrate it.

Sweet-swinging Rick Monday takes a cut against the Yankees during the 1981 World Series. *Photo courtesy of Focus on Sport/Getty Images.*

Johnny Podres arrived in Brooklyn in 1953, a brash, cocky, and bold kid of 20 years from upstate New York joining a veteran, championship team loaded with stars named Jackie Robinson, Gil Hodges, Roy Campanella, Pee Wee Reese, Carl Erskine, Preacher Roe, and Duke Snider. Podres was a rookie in name only. Unintimidated and unafraid, he meshed seamlessly with the older, established major leaguers, most of whom were anywhere from six to twelve years older than he was, and earned their respect by winning nine games and losing only four as the 1953 Dodgers won their second straight National League pennant by 13 games over the Milwaukee Braves.

If he was in awe of the players around him, if he was even aware of the magnitude of their accomplishments, it was never apparent. He was a Dodger in good standing. He was their peer. And he was accepted by them. They were his teammates, and they would become his friends.

Years later—long after he had earned his teammates' everlasting respect, acceptance, and gratitude by pitching and winning Game 7 of the 1955 World Series, a 2–0 victory over the Yankees to clinch Brooklyn's only world championship—Podres could look back nostalgically and reminisce about being one of the fabled Boys of Summer. He spoke respectfully about Robinson and Roe and lovingly about Gil, Campy, and his roommate, the Duke:

You saw it every day with Duke. They compared him with Willie Mays and Mickey Mantle. How can you be in that category if you weren't a great player? The song was "Willie, Mickey, and the Duke." Snider was third, but that didn't make any difference because they're all Hall of Famers. What difference does it make if you're third? You're still in the Hall.

I saw Duke make a lot of catches, but the greatest catch I ever saw was in Philadelphia in 1953 when he climbed the fence to take a home run away from [Willie] Puddin' Head Jones. Clem Labine was pitching and the bases were loaded, and Jones hit a drive to

Editor's note: Duke Snider was too humble to put himself on his list of all-time Dodgers center fielders, but any fan knows he belongs right at the top. Here he holds one bat for each home run hit in the first six games of the 1952 World Series against the Yankees.

left center. The ball was going over, and Duke dug his spikes in the wall, leaped, and caught it. He just took it away. What a catch! Saved the game.

Russ Meyer, our starting pitcher that day, ran all the way out to center field to shake Snider's hand. That's the fastest I ever saw Meyer run. You can talk about Willie Mays, but that was the greatest catch I ever saw.

Duke got a lot of big hits for me when I pitched. He was really good with me, and Erskine.

Charlie Dressen used to have a clubhouse meeting and he'd show Duke up in front of the whole team. If Charlie thought Duke wasn't hustling or something, he would take Duke apart all the time. He did it to get the best out of Duke, and after he'd get on him, Duke would go out and get three hits. After the game, Duke would walk by and make a gesture at Charlie as if to say, "I know why you got on me."

Every time Charlie got on him, Duke would go on a tear. He didn't want to be embarrassed again. Charlie got the best of him and Duke would sulk at times, but what a ballplayer he was. He could hit for average and hit for power. He could catch the ball, he could run, and he could throw. He could do everything. He and Don Zimmer got fined by Buzzie Bavasi because they had this competition where they tried to see who could throw a ball out of the stadium.

Duke had trouble with left-handers, so he would bunt against them. But we never saw many left-handers, especially in Brooklyn because we had so many powerful right-handed hitters. But Duke would wear out right-handers. He could hit Robin Roberts in his sleep, and Roberts, in his time, was probably the best pitcher in the game.

People who read that right field in Ebbets Field was only 296 feet away think it was an easy home-run park for left-handed hitters, but that's not true. The fence was 40 feet high, and when Duke hit them there, the ball was still going. The balls that he hit there would have been out in any ballpark.

What a great player Duke was. He could do it all.

For that action, Monday made headlines, got his name mentioned prominently in the papers, earned a lot of positive (and some negative) publicity, and was honored by the Illinois legislature with Rick Monday Day on May 4, 1976, for his act. He also managed to get himself traded.

There was no connection between the flag incident and the trade, but one year later, the Cubs dealt Monday to the Dodgers. Although his best years were behind him, Monday had enough left to help the Dodgers for a few years. He was a good, steady ballplayer. He had a beautiful swing and a desire to play, and he was fun to watch because he loved to play.

Eventually, a series of injuries shortened Rick's career and he retired. He became a broadcaster—and a good one—for the Dodgers, a job he still holds.

Had he played his entire career with the Dodgers, Hall of Famer **Max Carey** would be at the top of my list of the five greatest center fielders in team history instead of at the bottom. Just look at his career numbers: 2,665 hits and 738 stolen bases. As a base stealer, he was the National League equivalent of

Max Carey, shown here as the manager of the Brooklyn Dodgers, was also one of the franchise's best all-time center fielders.

Ty Cobb. Ten times he led the league in steals, but each of those times he was a member of the Pittsburgh Pirates.

A switch-hitting leadoff man with great speed, Carey was regarded as the best defensive center fielder of his era, the perennial league leader in putouts and total chances. His career total putouts is only exceeded by Willie Mays and Tris Speaker and his total chances by Mays, Speaker, and Cobb. He also holds the all-time National League record for assists by an outfielder, with 339.

By the time the Dodgers got him in 1926, Carey was 36 years old, his best days behind him. But he still stole 32 bases in 1927, second in the league to Frankie Frisch.

When his playing career was over, Carey took a job as a scout with the Pirates and then was brought back to Brooklyn as manager in 1932. Unfortunately, his managerial career was not as successful as his playing career. For one thing, he found himself in the unenviable position of replacing the popular Wilbert Robinson. Carey actually improved the team by two wins and finished in third place in 1932, but the following year the Dodgers dropped from 81 wins to 65 and finished in sixth place. As a result, Carey was fired as manager and replaced by Casey Stengel.

Statistical Summaries

All statistics are for player's Dodgers career only.

HITTING

G = Games

H = Hits

HR = Home runs

RBI = Runs batted in

SB = Stolen bases

BA = Batting average

Center Fielder	Years	G	H	HR	RBI	SB	BA
Pete Reiser *Hit three doubles and a home run against the Pirates on June 2, 1942*	1940–42 1946–48	616	666	44	298	78	.306
Willie Davis *Stole a record three bases in Game 5 of the 1965 World Series*	1960–73	1,952	2,091	154	849	335	.279
Brett Butler *Led NL in singles each season from 1990 to 1993*	1991–97	763	837	14	191	179	.298

continued	Years	G	H	HR	RBI	SB	BA
Rick Monday *Hit 11 home runs against Tom Seaver*	1977–84	645	387	73	226	8	.254
Max Carey *Had five or more hits in a single game nine times*	1926–29	298	249	3	81	50	.260

FIELDING

PO = Putouts

A = Assists

E = Errors

DP = Double plays

TC/G = Total chances divided by games played

FA = Fielding average

Center Fielder	PO	A	E	DP	TC/G	FA
Pete Reiser	1,151	41	26	4	2.4	.979
Willie Davis	4,436	123	105	17	2.4	.977
Brett Butler	1,666	36	6	10	2.3	.996
Rick Monday	712	13	15	0	1.8	.980
Max Carey	610	27	19	7	2.5	.971

EIGHT

Right Fielder

In 1947, the year I joined the Dodgers, our center fielder was a tough, hard-nosed player from Pennsylvania named **Carl Furillo**, one of the best center fielders in the game. In 1949 they put me in center field and moved Carl to right field, and he became an even greater right fielder than he was a center fielder.

Furillo could do it all, with the possible exception of run. He didn't steal many bases, but he didn't have to. He could hit, hit for power, catch the ball, and throw. Boy, could he throw! He was from Reading, Pennsylvania, and he had a cannon for an arm, so they nicknamed him "the Reading Rifle." He played the right-field wall in Ebbets Field like nobody else, and many times I saw that rifle arm gun runners out at first on hits that should have been singles.

1. CARL FURILLO

2. REGGIE SMITH

3. DIXIE WALKER

4. BABE HERMAN

5. FRANK HOWARD

On the right-field wall was the scoreboard, and at the bottom of the scoreboard was the Abe Stark sign. Stark owned a men's clothing store in Brooklyn, and he also became the borough president of Brooklyn. The sign was an advertising gimmick of his. It said, Hit Sign, Win Suit. In other words, any

Carl Furillo (center), posing with Roy Campanella (left) and Gil Hodges in 1952, had one of the strongest right-field arms of all time.

player that hit the sign on a fly (it actually would take a low line drive) would be given a free suit. I don't think Abe Stark ever gave away any suits. The sign was only about 5' tall, making it very difficult to hit. And with Furillo patrolling right field, hitting the sign was almost impossible.

Carl saved Stark so many suits by catching line drives headed for the sign that he figured he was entitled to a free suit for his efforts, so he went to Stark to plead his case. Stark argued that Furillo was only doing the job he was being paid to do by the Dodgers. But Carl kept insisting that he was saving Stark a lot of money, so they arrived at a compromise. Furillo got a free pair of slacks.

Carl had a lifetime batting average of .299 for 15 years, more than 1,000 RBIs, and almost 200 home runs—not to mention his great defense—better numbers than some guys who are in the Hall of Fame.

You never hear Furillo's name mentioned when they talk about players who should be considered for the Hall of Fame. Why? I don't know, because Carl had a lifetime batting average of .299 for 15 years, more than 1,000 RBIs, and almost 200 home runs —not to mention his great defense—better numbers than some guys who are in the Hall of Fame. Furillo hit 20 or more home runs in a season three times in his career, and he drove in more than 100 runs twice and 90 or more six times.

I once asked him, "Skoonj [that was his nickname because he loved the Italian delicacy scungilli], when you come to bat and you see those runners in scoring position, what do you think about?"

He said, "When I see those guys on base, I see dollar signs. If I drive in 100 runs, it's dollars in my pocket."

Furillo was an outstanding but underrated ballplayer. I always thought he was the most underrated of all the Dodgers from my time. You had to see him every day to really appreciate him. He was so easy to play alongside of. He knew how to play the game. We developed a great rapport in the outfield. On a ball hit to right center, Carl would take it if it was hit deep, and I would take it if it was hit shallow. We had it worked out so that there was never anything even close to a collision between us.

Carl was the best right fielder I ever saw until Roberto Clemente came along, and Clemente is possibly the best ballplayer I've ever seen. And just think that we could have had Clemente in our outfield.

The Dodgers signed Clemente as a teenager out of Puerto Rico and tried to hide him in the minor leagues. The rule back then was that if you signed a player for a bonus of $4,000 or more, he had to stay on the major league roster for two full seasons. The Dodgers already had Sandy Koufax on their roster, and they didn't want to carry two kids and essentially play the season with only 23 players, so they sent Clemente to Montreal. With Clemente went orders to play him only occasionally, and out of position, so the major league scouts wouldn't see how much ability he had.

But they couldn't fool Branch Rickey, who by then had moved on from the Dodgers to the Pirates. Rickey sent Clyde Sukeforth to Montreal to look at Clemente, and Sukey came back raving about the young Puerto Rican. The Pirates drafted Clemente and got one of the greatest players ever to play the game.

Imagine if the Dodgers had Clemente all those years. I don't know if Clemente would have played left and Furillo right, or if Furillo would have moved to left to allow Clemente to play right. Either of them could have been a great left fielder, and that would have given us a terrific outfield for years. With both of them, we might have won a few more world championships in Brooklyn.

Getting back to Furillo, he was steady, and when he put his uniform on, he meant business. He was a fierce competitor who burned with the desire to win and could beat you in so many ways. He seemed to have a hatred for anybody in an opponent's uniform.

After Leo Durocher left the Dodgers and became manager of the Giants, he and Furillo had an ongoing feud. Leo liked to taunt Carl from the bench, as he did every opposing player, and Carl always resented the fact that when Leo managed the Dodgers, he platooned Furillo. Carl hated that because he wanted to play every day and felt he deserved to play every day.

In 1953 Furillo won the National League batting title with a .344 average. But in a September game with the Giants, Carl was hit on the wrist by a pitch from Ruben Gomez. Furillo was certain Durocher had ordered the pitch because when he managed the Dodgers he did the same sort of thing to the Giants. Carl tried to get at Gomez and was stopped by the umpires, but when he got to first base, Furillo heard Durocher yelling at him from the Giants dugout. Carl took off after Durocher, and as he did, he heard umpire Babe Pinelli shouting, "Get him, Carl, get him!"

hey were four young outfielders, each born two years apart: Gene Hermanski the oldest, Carl Furillo two years younger, George "Shotgun" Shuba two years younger than Furillo, and Duke Snider the youngest. They all came to the Brooklyn Dodgers in the magical forties.

Furillo and Snider would settle in at right and center fields, respectively, teammates and outfield partners for years and among the brightest stars in the Dodgers firmament. Hermanski was expected to take left field, joining Snider and Furillo in the outfield, but was eventually traded to the Cubs for veteran Andy Pafko. Shuba had his shot at filling the left-field position, but a chronically bad knee reduced his effectiveness and he never lived up to the promise he had shown as he rose through the Dodgers' minor league system.

Nonetheless, Shuba was a witness to, and a participant in, history. He was a member of the Montreal Royals in 1946 when Jackie Robinson officially broke baseball's long-standing, infamous, and shameful color line. What's more, Shuba helped to create another historic baseball moment involving the color barrier.

The scene is captured in a widely circulated, famous photograph titled "A Handshake for the Century." The date is April 18, 1946, Robinson's first game in organized baseball. The setting is Roosevelt Stadium in Jersey City, New Jersey. The photo shows Robinson crossing home plate after hitting a home run and Shuba, No. 13 on the back of his uniform, grasping his teammate's hand in a congratulatory handshake, which was customary at the time. It was the first time in baseball history that a white man shook the hand of a black man on a baseball field.

"Jackie batted second in the lineup, and I batted third," Shuba vividly recalls. "When he hit the home run, I naturally shook his hand. I didn't think anything of it at the time. I'm from Youngstown, Ohio. I grew up playing with a lot of black ballplayers. Over the years people have asked me if I felt funny shaking the hand of a black man. Hell, I couldn't care less if he was purple. He was on our team."

While the focus was on Robinson on the Opening Day of the season, Shuba took the spotlight on the second day by hitting three home runs for the Royals.

"I didn't want to do it on the first day," Shuba says. "That day belonged to Jackie. So I waited until the second day to hit the three home runs . . . and if you believe that, I have a bridge I'd like to sell you."

Two years later Shuba arrived in Brooklyn and was again Robinson's teammate, this time as one of the Boys of Summer.

"I remember Jackie was getting death threats," Shuba said. "He got a letter from some guy who said he was going to shoot Robinson when he went onto the field. That gave Gene Hermanski an idea. He told Jackie everybody would wear his number, No. 42, so the guy would not know which one to shoot.

"And Jackie said, 'I'm afraid he'll still be able to pick me out.'"

In Brooklyn Shuba also was reunited with his outfield buddies, Snider and Furillo. Shuba fondly remembers that time:

I first met Carl in spring training in 1946 in Daytona Beach. The Dodgers had bought Furillo from the Reading club [Editor's note: According to Buzzie Bavasi, "Larry MacPhail sent me to Reading to buy the club. For $5,000 we received the club, a set of uniforms, a broken down bus, and three players, including Furillo."], and we were both on the Montreal roster, but Carl never came to Montreal. He went right to Brooklyn, and I went to Montreal.

Furillo was well-liked by everybody, a straight shooter, and a tough guy who played hurt. He was a good fielder with a great arm. Nobody around could play the right-field wall in Ebbets Field like he could. Right field in Ebbets Field was the sun field—tough to play, but Carl mastered it. Also, right field sloped down, so if you had to make a throw to third base, you were throwing uphill. But Furillo had such a great arm, he never had any trouble throwing to third base.

Carl was also a great hitter. He led the league in hitting in 1953. That was the year he had his hand broken when he got into a fight late in the year against the Giants at the Polo Grounds. Ruben Gomez hit him with a pitch, and Carl blamed Leo Durocher. He started yelling at Leo, "You called that pitch. I'm going to get you."

> *The next thing you knew, Carl was going into the Giants dugout after Leo. Somebody—I'm not going to say who—said, "Let's form a circle and let them go at it and get the bad blood out." Instead, there was a scramble in the dugout as Furillo tried to get at Durocher, and somebody stepped on Carl's hand and he wound up with a broken bone in his hand.*
>
> *I remember one time, somebody hit a line drive to right field that should have been a single, but Carl grabbed the ball on one hop and fired to first and threw the guy out.*
>
> *When I played left field, I was playing alongside two outfielders with great arms, Snider and Furillo. So I would cheat and move in a few steps because I wanted to look good next to those guys if I had to make a throw.*

Furillo dived into a pile of bodies on the Giants bench, trying to get at Durocher. In the melee, a Giants player stepped on Furillo's hand and broke his finger, sidelining him for the rest of the season. Carl never forgave Durocher.

As much as Furillo hated Durocher, he also hated Sal Maglie when Sal was a Giant. They called Maglie "the Barber" because he liked to shave hitters (throw up and in on them) to intimidate them. Many times Furillo was knocked down by Maglie, and there was no love lost between them. But when Maglie came to the Dodgers, Carl was one of the first guys to welcome him to the club. Furillo put his arm around Sal and said, "Now get somebody out like you got us out."

Furillo wasn't a buddy-buddy type of guy. He wouldn't socialize with the other players very much. He'd come to our parties once in a while, but he lived in a different part of Brooklyn than the rest of us did, and he had his own friends. Carl was a bit of a loner. He was different, but he was a great teammate, and once he put that uniform on, he was a member of the team, and he played hard.

Furillo and the Dodgers came to an unfortunate parting of the ways after the team moved to Los Angeles. He sued the Dodgers after they released him when he was injured. He got $21,000 in a settlement of the suit, but he also got a reputation. As a result, he never got another job in baseball, with the Dodgers or any other team, which was too bad. Carl would have been a great coach. He had so much to teach young players about how to field, how to hit, and how to win.

Reggie Smith will be remembered as one of the best switch-hitters the game has ever seen. *Photo courtesy of Focus on Sport/Getty Images.*

I have nothing but the highest regard for **Reggie Smith** as a baseball player and as a man. He wasn't a Dodger for very long, only five and a half seasons, but he made his mark in Los Angeles, which was, and still is, his home.

Reggie was a great high school athlete in both football and baseball. He could throw with either hand, and, of course, he became one of the best switch-hitters baseball ever saw. When he retired, he had hit more home runs (314) than any switch-hitter except Mickey Mantle. He was also the first switch-hitter to hit at least 100 home runs in both the National League and the American League and to hit a home run from each side of the plate in the same game, a feat he accomplished twice in each league. (Editor's note: Eddie Murray, for one, has accomplished both feats.)

By the time he came to the Dodgers in a trade with the Cardinals in June 1976, Reggie had already done great things in Boston and St. Louis. But he also came with a reputation for being something of a malcontent. Like many reputations ballplayers pick up early in their careers, I found Reggie's to be the farthest thing from the truth. Perhaps he had mellowed by the time he got to the Dodgers (he was then in his thirties), or maybe it's simply that people misunderstood his fierce competitiveness.

Reggie Smith was very close to the type of competitor Jackie Robinson was. When the umpire said, "Play ball," he was out there to beat you. In 1977 he joined with Steve Garvey, Ron Cey, and Dusty Baker as the first four teammates to hit at least 30 home runs in a season. And he was a big part of the group that won three pennants and one World Series with the Dodgers in five years.

Injuries shortened Reggie's career, and he opened a hitting school in the Los Angeles area that he still runs. He's the best hitting instructor I've ever seen, and he's a super guy and a good friend.

Mention the name "Babe" in baseball circles and the one and only Babe Ruth immediately comes to mind. But Ruth wasn't the "one and only" Babe in baseball during his time, and he wasn't even number one to Brooklyn fans, who had a Babe of their own.

Floyd Caves "Babe" Herman came to the Dodgers in 1926 when "the other Babe" was in the prime of his career with the Yankees, just a few miles away. Obviously, Ruth got most of the attention and acclaim and clearly was the winner of the "Battle of the Babes" during the six years (1926–1931) they coexisted in New York City.

In that six-year period, Ruth hit 302 home runs, an average of 50.3 per year, and drove in 921 runs, an average of 153.5. But Brooklyn's Babe was no slouch. He belted 111 homers in those six years with the Dodgers, an average of 18.5, and drove in 585 runs, an average of 97.5. And he outhit Ruth for average in three of those six seasons.

Herman's biggest year was 1930, when he hit 35 homers (Ruth hit 49) and knocked in 130 runs (Ruth drove in 153). But Herman batted .393 that season, to Ruth's .359. It's interesting to note, and a sign of the times, that even

Babe Herman, shown here as a member of the Pittsburgh Pirates in 1935, coexisted in New York with baseball's other Babe for six seasons and held his own against the Bambino statistically.

with a lifetime average of .324 for 13 years and three seasons with an average of .340 or better, Herman never won a batting title. The year he hit .393, Bill Terry of the Giants won the batting crown with a .401 average, the last National Leaguer to hit .400.

Nevertheless, Herman's .393 average, 241 hits, 416 total bases, 94 extra-base hits, 143 runs, .678 slugging percentage, and .455 on-base percentage in 1930 still stand as all-time Dodgers records, and it's amazing to me that the man is not in the Hall of Fame.

Because of the staggering home-run numbers Ruth put up, Herman's 35 homers in 1935 might not seem like much, but, believe me, in 1930 it was. To that point, that number had been reached only seven times in National League history and was a record for the Dodgers. The record would last for 21 years, until Gil Hodges hit 40 in 1951.

Herman's first season in Brooklyn was Zack Wheat's last, and Babe replaced Wheat as the offensive leader of the Dodgers. He also typified the Dodgers' Daffiness Boys of the twenties and thirties.

"I wasn't the world's greatest fielder," Herman once said, "but I was a pretty fair country hitter."

Herman was being modest, on both counts. He led the National League in errors in consecutive seasons, as a first baseman in 1927 and as an outfielder in 1928. Apparently, hard as they tried, the Dodgers couldn't find a defensive position at which to hide him.

But a "pretty fair country hitter," I'll say.

If there's one thing for which Herman is best remembered, it's something for which he was blameless. He once doubled into a double play. Herman came to bat with the bases loaded and drove one against the right-field wall in Ebbets Field. Hank DeBerry, the runner on third, scored. The runner on second, Dazzy Vance, held up, then rounded third and headed home. The runner on first, Chick Fewster, stopped at third. When the outfielder threw home, Vance headed back to third. At the same time, Herman, running with his head down, slid into third, and the Dodgers had three men on third base. Herman was credited with a double and called out for passing a runner on the base paths.

The incident gave birth to an oft-quoted quip that was rehashed for years:

"The Dodgers have three men on base."

"Yeah? Which base?"

I got to know Herman a little bit when I was a kid. I was about 17 or 18 years old and he was scouting for the Pirates and tried to sign me. He told me he liked my swing, which was a nice compliment coming from a man who had a lifetime average of .324 for 13 major league seasons. The Pirates' offer was tempting, but I decided to sign with the Dodgers because they were my favorite team, even though the Pirates offered more money.

Unfortunately, the name **Dixie Walker** brings up some very unpleasant and distasteful memories. He was the ringleader of a group of Dodgers, all of them from the South, who objected to Jackie Robinson joining the team in 1947 and even signed a petition stating their objection and unwillingness to play on the same team as a black man. To his credit, Leo Durocher told Walker what he could do with his petition, and Robinson was welcomed by most, if not all, of the Dodgers.

I was never asked to sign the petition because I was a rookie with no standing on the team. I wouldn't have signed it anyway; I wasn't raised to believe that people of color were inferior to whites. But, then again, I wasn't raised in the South.

In Dixie's defense, it was a cultural thing. He was born and brought up in Georgia at a time when racism was rampant. It's all he ever knew. It must have been ingrained in him from childhood that blacks were inferior to whites and if that's what you grow up with, it stays with you, in many cases, forever.

After his initial attempted boycott of Robinson, Dixie backed off his position slightly as the season went on. He even occasionally gave batting tips to Robinson. I imagine that he looked at it not as helping a black man, but as helping a teammate for a common cause. And they were united in their desire to help the Dodgers win a pennant, which we did. Jackie was National League Rookie of the Year, and Dixie batted .306 and drove in 94 runs.

Later Walker became a minor league manager and a batting instructor for the Cardinals, Braves, and Dodgers. In that capacity, he worked with many black ballplayers and helped them with their hitting. But the stigma of that petition against Jackie Robinson stayed with him forever. It's an old, familiar story. An attack on someone often makes page one of the newspaper, while the retraction winds up buried deep in the back of the paper and never catches up with, or gets the same attention as, the original story.

Dixie Walker is shown warming up his arm before a game at Ebbets Field in 1946. *Photo courtesy of Time & Life Pictures/Getty Images.*

Frank Howard is shown as a member of the Washington Senators in 1968; he is about to connect on his eighth home run in five games, breaking a record set by Babe Ruth in 1921.

Taking that petition around and asking other players to sign it is to Walker's everlasting shame, but I have nothing but good things to say about Dixie Walker as a hitter. He came to Brooklyn in 1936, after floundering around and failing with the Yankees, White Sox, and Tigers, and became a big favorite in Brooklyn. So big a favorite, in fact, he picked up the Brooklynese nickname "the Peepuls Cherce."

In 1940, his first full year with the Dodgers, Walker batted .308, and he hit better than .300 in seven of the eight seasons he was a Dodger, with a high of .357 in 1944, when he won the batting title. The following year, he led the National League in RBIs with 124. He didn't hit a lot of home runs—his high was 13—but he was a great line-drive hitter, what baseball people call "a pure hitter." In 18 big-league seasons, he had more than 2,000 hits and a lifetime average of .306.

> *[Walker] didn't hit a lot of home runs—his high was 13—but he was a great line-drive hitter, what baseball people call "a pure hitter." In 18 big-league seasons, he had more than 2,000 hits and a lifetime average of .306.*

Walker helped the Dodgers win pennants in 1941 and 1947, but his greatest contribution to the Dodgers might have been in getting traded to Pittsburgh after the 1947 season. In that deal, we got Preacher Roe and Billy Cox.

125

Frank Howard was so much fun to be around, and he still is. He had some shortcomings as a player—he couldn't run, wasn't a very good fielder, struck out too much, and couldn't hit Stu Miller with a fly swatter—but nobody worked harder and nobody hit the ball any harder than Frank.

I can still see a couple balls he hit off Whitey Ford in the 1963 World Series: a line drive in Game 1 that was almost caught by shortstop Tony Kubek but took off like a rocket and hit the left-center-field wall in Yankee Stadium for a double, and a tremendous home run in Game 4 at Dodger Stadium that landed in the upper deck.

One night we were in Cincinnati and I was leading off third. Howard hooked a line drive foul that hit me on the shoulder, bounced up, and hit me on the ear. The next thing I remembered I was sitting in the coach's box.

After the 1964 season, the Dodgers traded Howard to Washington, which turned out to be a good deal for the Dodgers. They got Claude Osteen in return. Meanwhile, with the Senators, Frank won two American League home-run championships and one RBI title. He finished his career with 382 homers and 1,119 RBIs. In the 12 years from 1960 to 1971, he averaged 30 homers and 87 RBIs per year.

"Hondo"—he got that nickname from the John Wayne movie about the cowboy Hondo—had been an All-American basketball player at Ohio State in the fifties. He's 6'7", which in those days was big, even for a basketball player. As a baseball player, he was gigantic.

We used to kid him that somebody must have taken his classes for him. And sure enough, one night in Cincinnati we were warming up for the game and some guy came down near the field and yelled to me, "Hey, Duke, where's Frank Howard? I went to school with him at Ohio State. Where is he? I want to say hello to him."

"He's right there; I'm warming up with him," I said, and I pointed to big Frank.

The guy did a double take and said, "That's not the Frank Howard that I had a class with. The guy I had a class with was 5'6" and had glasses."

We never let Frank hear the end of that one.

Somebody once said that Howard is living proof that God is good because as big as Howard is, if he were a mean person, he could cause a lot of destruction. But Frank doesn't have a mean bone in his body. As big as he is, that's how gentle and lovable he is. A big old teddy bear, he's one of the nicest, most sincere, and most polite people one could ever meet.

Statistical Summaries

All statistics are for player's Dodgers career only.

HITTING

G = Games
H = Hits
HR = Home runs
RBI = Runs batted in
SB = Stolen bases
BA = Batting average

Right Fielder	Years	G	H	HR	RBI	SB	BA
Carl Furillo *One more hit would have given him a .300 career average*	1946–60	1,806	1,910	192	1,058	48	.299
Reggie Smith *Had league-leading .427 on-base percentage in 1977*	1976–81	542	516	97	301	32	.297
Dixie Walker *One-third of .300-hitting outfield with Medwick and Reiser in 1941*	1940–47	1,207	1,395	67	725	44	.311

continued	Years	G	H	HR	RBI	SB	BA
Babe Herman *Collected 77 extra-base hits to lead NL in 1931*	1926–31 1945	888	1,093	112	594	69	.339
Frank Howard *Hit first career homer on September 10, 1958, against Robin Roberts*	1958–64	624	567	123	382	3	.269

FIELDING

PO = Putouts

A = Assists

E = Errors

DP = Double plays

TC/G = Total chances divided by games played

FA = Fielding average

Right Fielder	PO	A	E	DP	TC/G	FA
Carl Furillo	3,322	151	74	34	2.0	.979
Reggie Smith	902	38	22	11	2.0	.977
Dixie Walker	2,386	117	67	29	2.2	.974
Babe Herman	1,073	60	54	12	1.9	.955
Frank Howard	838	40	27	5	1.6	.970

NINE

Right-Handed Pitcher

This, for me, is the toughest category to rate because I'm limited to picking only five right-handed pitchers, and the Dodgers have had so many great ones that it's almost impossible to eliminate any of them. Just look at the 20-game winners alone—a dying breed in the modern game—that don't make my list: Whitlow Wyatt, Kirby Higbe, Luke "Hot Potato" Hamlin, Ralph Branca, Bill Singer, Andy Messersmith, Don Sutton (a career 300-game winner and a Hall of Famer), Orel Hershiser (who pitched 59 consecutive scoreless innings in 1988 and broke Don Drysdale's major league record streak by one inning), and Ramon Martinez.

But a rule is a rule, and because I can only pick five, that's what I'll do. And I don't apologize for the five I picked, all of whom were 20-game winners and three of whom are in the Hall of Fame.

At the top of my list is Big D, **Don Drysdale**, one of the fiercest competitors I have ever known. Don hated to lose—at anything. He didn't even like to hear the word *lose*. I got into it with him once in, of all things, a fantasy camp game. I was umpiring and he was managing one of the teams, and I made a call that went against his team. Don

1. Don Drysdale

2. Don Newcombe

3. Dazzy Vance

4. Burleigh Grimes

5. Carl Erskine

was seething. As he walked off the field he passed me and said, "Too bad they don't have a line in the box score for losing umpire."

Drysdale had the reputation of being a headhunter, which is an exaggeration. Well, maybe only a slight exaggeration. Don wasn't always trying to hit batters, but he didn't hesitate to throw inside, which a pitcher has to do to be successful, and he didn't mind capitalizing on his reputation to get an edge. He even helped perpetuate that reputation. He would walk up to Mickey Mantle before a World Series game, pinch him on the hip or around the ribs, and say, "Well, Mick, where would you like one today?"

One time, Walter Alston ordered Drysdale to give Frank Robinson an intentional walk. Don hit Robby with the first pitch and later said, "I figured, why waste three pitches?"

Drysdale had the reputation of being a headhunter, which is an exaggeration. Well, maybe only a slight exaggeration. Don wasn't always trying to hit batters, but he didn't hesitate to throw inside, which a pitcher has to do to be successful, and he didn't mind capitalizing on his reputation to get an edge.

Five times Drysdale led the National League in hit batters, and he finished his career with a modern National League record 154 notches on his belt—154 hit batsmen. Don't get the idea that Big D was more bluster than talent or that he succeeded mainly through intimidation. He was a tremendous pitcher who once won 25 games, and another time 23, and finished with 209 victories in his 14 seasons, all with the Dodgers, on his way to the Hall of Fame. Three times he led the league in strikeouts. He pitched 49 shutouts, and in 1968 he pitched six consecutive shutouts and set a major league record—later broken by another Dodger, Orel Hershiser—with 58⅔ consecutive scoreless innings. (Editor's note: Official baseball statistics do not recognize thirds of an inning by pitchers, so Drysdale's record went into the books as 58 consecutive scoreless innings.)

Drysdale was a workhorse. He never missed a start, and in four straight years, 1962 to 1965, he pitched more than 300 innings and led the league in starts, with 41, 42, 40, and 42.

As if that wasn't enough, Drysdale also was one of the best-hitting pitchers in baseball history. He led National League pitchers in home runs four times, twice tying the league record with 7, and his 29 career home runs is second all-time in National League history to Warren Spahn. In 1965 Drysdale not only won 23 games, but he also batted .300, hit seven homers, had a slugging percentage of .508, and was used often as a pinch-hitter.

Drysdale came to the Brooklyn Dodgers in 1956. The next year, at age 21, he won 17 games. Later, in Los Angeles, he teamed with Sandy Koufax to

Don Drysdale lets one fly during a game against the New York Mets at Shea Stadium on
June 7, 1964.

give the Dodgers perhaps the best one-two pitching punch in baseball history, certainly the best in their era. Drysdale and Koufax not only terrorized National League batters during the sixties, but they also became close friends and even entered into an agreement to stage a joint holdout after the 1965 season. That was before agents, free agency, and arbitration.

Don and Sandy had combined to win 49 games, and figuring there was strength in numbers, they got together to ask for a three-year contract for $1.05 million, to be divided equally between them. Imagine what they could get today! But the Dodgers refused to give in to the joint demands, and Koufax and Drysdale wound up signing separate one-year deals, Drysdale's for $110,000.

When he retired during the 1969 season, an era ended. Drysdale was the last Dodger who had played in Brooklyn.

Don Newcombe gets a bad rap. They say he didn't win the big games, but he won 123 games for the Dodgers, and believe me, he won some very big games. Big, big games.

Newk won 17 games in his first season, 1949, and was voted National League Rookie of the Year. He won 19 games in 1950, 20 in 1951, 20 in 1955, and 27 in 1956 and was named the National League's Most Valuable Player. He also won the first Cy Young Award, when only one was awarded, not two—one to a pitcher in each league—as they do now.

The reason for Newcombe's bad rap is that he never won a World Series game or a playoff game, but let's look a little closer. In 1949, his rookie year, Newcombe started Game 1 of the World Series against the Yankees in Yankee Stadium and pitched eight shutout innings, allowing just four hits. Unfortunately for Newk, Allie Reynolds shut us out on two hits, and in the bottom of the ninth Tommy Henrich led off with a line-drive home run into the short right-field porch, making Newcombe the hard-luck, 1–0 loser. Don could have easily won that game if we had given him any run support.

In 1950 we came to the final game of the season one game behind the Phillies. If we had beaten the Phillies, we'd have forced a playoff. The main reason we were even in that position is that Newcombe practically carried us in the last month of the season. On September 6, in Philadelphia, he started both games of a doubleheader against the Phillies. He went all the way in the

Don Newcombe (right) gets a show of appreciation from his battery mate, Roy Campanella, after Newcombe shut out the Giants on September 2, 1949.

first game and shut out the Phillies 2–0. In the second game, he left in the seventh inning, trailing 2–0. We rallied to win, but Newk wasn't involved in the decision. That was another time we let him down by not giving him enough run support. He could have won both games of the doubleheader; he certainly pitched well enough to do so.

The only pitcher to start both ends of a doubleheader since Newcombe did it is Wilbur Wood of the Chicago White Sox in 1973, but Wood threw a knuckleball, which doesn't put a great deal of stress on a pitcher's arm. Newcombe, on the other hand, was a power pitcher who left it all out there with every pitch. Besides, Wood lost both games to the Yankees.

And, as I said, no pitcher has started both games of a doubleheader since. I know they don't play doubleheaders anymore, but if they did, can you imagine a pitcher starting both games? The manager would immediately get a call from the pitcher's agent, lawyer, union leader, even the team owner.

Ralph Branca and Don Newcombe are linked in baseball history by one infamous inning in one memorable game, the historic ninth inning of the third playoff game between the Brooklyn Dodgers and the New York Giants on October 3, 1951. But the relationship between Branca, big No. 13, and Big Newk goes beyond one inning of one game. Branca was already a 21-game winner and a six-year veteran of the major league baseball wars at the age of 23 when Newcombe arrived in Brooklyn in 1949.

Branca talks about their time playing together:

We were buddies and partners. We worked out together. We teamed up to play pepper and to run sprints. We were both big guys [Branca 6'3" and 220 pounds, Newcombe 6'4" and 220 pounds], and they used to say that big guys had to do more work to stay in shape, which is a bunch of nonsense, but we did it anyway. We'd run 20 laps together on our own, and then the pitching coach would come out and we'd have to run 10 more laps.

Newcombe was a great pitcher, and a workhorse. He'd take the ball every fourth day, and he'd pitch in relief. In 1951 Charlie Dressen wore us out in the stretch. In the last 50 games it seemed like one of us was in just about every game. [Editor's note: Newcombe and Branca started 31 of the Dodgers' last 62 games; Branca also pitched in relief 15 times that season, had 13 complete games, and logged 204 innings; Newcombe relieved four times, pitched 18 complete games, and threw 272 innings.] By the end of the season, we were both worn out.

But Newk was a horse. He never missed a start, and he won 20 games that year. He had this short curveball. I compare it to the pitch Mariano Rivera throws. Today, they call it a cutter. I called it a spiral.

Branca remembers the day in Philadelphia in 1950 when Newcombe started both games of a doubleheader against the Phillies, and Branca figures he had something to do with Newcombe's iron-man act:

I talked him into it. He won the first game and he said to me, "Now, they need somebody else for the second game." The plan was for Newcombe to come back and pitch the next day.

I said, "Newk, don't do that. You'll stiffen up tomorrow. You're better off pitching the second game, while you're loose. Take a shower, change your shirt, and go out there and pitch. Make believe it's an extra-inning game." And that's what he did. Almost won the second game too. He left after seven innings, trailing 2–0, but we came back to win the game.

Branca scoffs at the notion that Newcombe couldn't win the big game.

First game of the 1949 World Series, he loses 1–0. The Dodgers got only two hits off Allie Reynolds. That's not Newcombe's fault. In the third game of the playoffs in 1951, Newcombe started for the fourth time in 12 days. He pitched his heart out. He held the Giants to four hits through eight innings, but he was worn out and the Giants got to him in the ninth. That's when I came in.

When I got to the mound, I said, "I'll save it for you, Newk," and he patted me on the back and left.

All the world knows what happened next—Bobby Thomson's shot heard 'round the world.

"Later," said Branca, "Newcombe said, 'You saved it for me, all right!'"

Newk started the final game in 1950 on three days' rest, and after nine innings, the score was tied, 1–1. We had a runner thrown out at the plate in the bottom of the ninth. If that run had scored, we'd have won the game 2–1, forced a playoff, and Newcombe would have had his 20th win of the season, and he would have been a big hero. But it didn't happen, and in the tenth, Dick Sisler hit a three-run homer to beat us, so Newk was the goat. Again, we didn't give him enough run support.

In 1951 Newcombe won 20 games. That was the year we finished the regular season tied with the Giants, which required a three-game playoff. Newk helped us get to that point by winning his 19th game on September 26, and then coming back with only two days' rest to win his 20th, a 5–0 shutout.

Dazzy Vance shows off his form during spring training in Clearwater, Florida, on March 3, 1932.

So, when he started Game 3 against the Giants, he was pitching with only three days' rest. Still, he went into the bottom of the ninth leading 4–1. You probably remember what happened next: a scratch single by Alvin Dark, a seeing-eye single by Don Mueller, an opposite-field double by Whitey Lockman, and then Ralph Branca replaced Newcombe to face Bobby Thomson. Do I have to go any further?

After that, Newcombe was awful in the World Series. He lost Game 1 in 1955 and was hammered in Game 7 in 1956, and that's what people remember, his failure in the World Series. They forget all the other things. They forget how he carried us on his back, with three 20-win seasons and 112 wins in six years. They forget his iron-man performance of starting both games of a doubleheader. They forget that not only was he our ace and a big-game pitcher during the regular season, but he also was an outstanding hitter who had a lifetime average of .271, tied the National League record for home runs by a pitcher with seven in 1955, and hit two home runs in a single game three times in his career. When his arm went dead, he even went to play in Japan as a first baseman.

Newk isn't in the Hall of Fame, and I wonder why. I'm not saying that his record in the major leagues warrants him being elected, but for years they have put players from the Negro Leagues into a special wing of the Hall of Fame, and Newcombe's name has never come up. He played only one year in the Negro Leagues, but I'm still confused. The MVP, the Cy Young Award, the three 20-win seasons—Newcombe did all that in the big leagues, but he was never close to getting into the Hall of Fame. The Negro Leagues players who did get in never came close to doing what Newk did in the big leagues.

I remember meeting **Dazzy Vance** one time early in my career. He came to Ebbets Field for a game, and I was introduced to him. It was a brief meeting, and I have only a vague recollection of it. We really didn't have much of a conversation, which I regret. Looking back, I realize that I would have liked to talk to him about his pitching philosophy and about what the game was like in his day, but I didn't take advantage of the opportunity when I had it. I certainly knew who he was then, but it wasn't until much later that I found out more about him.

Vance didn't get to the major leagues to stay until he was 31 years old and had pitched in the minor leagues for 10 years. (Editor's note: he did have brief stints at ages 24 and 27.) When he got to Brooklyn in 1922, he more than made up for lost time. He won 197 games; struck out 2,045 batters; pitched 30 shutouts; won 20 or more games three times; led the league in strikeouts seven times, wins twice, and earned run average three times; pitched until he was 44; and was elected to the Hall of Fame.

The Dodgers actually were forced, against their better judgment, to take Vance. They wanted catcher Hank DeBerry from New Orleans, but the owners of the New Orleans club refused to separate DeBerry and Vance and insisted that if the Dodgers wanted the catcher, they also had to take the pitcher.

The Dodgers got lucky. While DeBerry, used mostly as a backup by the Dodgers, was a serviceable catcher for 11 years, Vance, who up to that time was best known for his wildness and a chronic sore arm, became a star and the dominant strikeout pitcher of the twenties.

Beginning in 1922, his first year with the Dodgers, Vance led the National League in strikeouts a record seven straight years. After winning 18 games for the Dodgers in each of his first two seasons, Vance hit it big in 1924, when he led the league with 28 wins, a 2.16 ERA, 30 complete games, and 262 strikeouts—127 more than the runner-up, his teammate Burleigh Grimes. For his amazing season, Vance was voted winner of the Chalmers Award, the forerunner to Most Valuable Player, over Rogers Hornsby, who batted an astounding .424 for the Cardinals.

Vance's stock-in-trade were a high leg kick followed by a waggle of his left foot, after which would come a blazing fastball, and a bagful of tricks he acquired through his years of experience, not the least of which was wearing a bright red undershirt with the sleeves tattered as a means of distracting the batter. That practice was eventually outlawed.

In addition to his pitching prowess, Vance was known for his vital contribution to the team known as the Daffiness Boys. He was one of three Dodgers who simultaneously landed on third base in a game against the Braves in 1926 (Editor's note: see the chapter on right fielders); thus the name, *Dazzy* (his given name was Clarence Arthur).

After winning 12 games in 1932, Vance was traded to the Cardinals, where he teamed up with the Dean brothers, giving the Cardinals a pitching staff that included a Dizzy, a Dazzy, and a Daffy.

Burleigh Grimes is best remembered as the last of baseball's legal spitball pitchers and one of the worst managers the Dodgers ever had, which is a great disservice to a man who pitched in the major leagues for 19 seasons, won 270 games, struck out 1,512 batters, pitched 35 shutouts, and was elected to the Hall of Fame. It's for his pitching record, not his managing log, that Grimes makes my list of the top five right-handed pitchers in Dodgers history.

Grimes broke into the major leagues with Pittsburgh in 1916, when pitchers were allowed to apply foreign substances to the ball. Grimes' modus operandi was to chew slippery elm to increase his saliva, which he then applied to the ball, causing it to dip and dive crazily and elude the bat. The elm irritated Burleigh's skin, so he wouldn't shave for two or three days before he pitched. Consequently, he took the mound with a few days' growth of beard, which gave him a menacing look and the nickname Ol' Stubblebeard.

In 1920 baseball outlawed the spitball for several reasons: it was deemed an unfair advantage for pitchers over hitters; the lords of baseball perceived that

Burleigh Grimes, shown here as the Dodgers' manager in 1937 alongside New York's Bill Terry, was best known for his spitball and his surly disposition on the mound.

fans wanted more offense in the game; it was unsightly and unsanitary; and it represented a danger to batters who, at the time, did not wear helmets. However, as a condition of the ban, those who were known to throw the pitch were allowed to continue to use it so as not to deprive them of their livelihood. At the time, there were 17 spitball pitchers in the major leagues. One by one, they retired, but Grimes hung around until 1934, 14 years after the ban was implemented. In that time, Grimes won 236 games, 158 for the Dodgers, which is sixth on their all-time list; led the National League in wins twice; and won 20 games or more five times.

From all reports, Grimes was mean on the mound, a guy who would throw at hitters to gain an advantage (think of Sal Maglie, Don Drysdale, Bob Gibson, Early Wynn, and from today, Pedro Martinez). They used to say that Grimes' idea of an intentional walk was one pitch at the batter's head instead of four to the outside.

In 1937 Grimes was brought back to Brooklyn as manager to replace Casey Stengel. It was thought that he would bring his fire to the team and that it would motivate and improve the Dodgers. The experiment was a failure, as Grimes' record in his two years was 131–171, with sixth- and seventh-place finishes.

In fairness to Grimes' managerial stint, he was constantly being undermined by the front office. In 1938 they brought in Babe Ruth as a coach and Leo Durocher as shortstop. Ruth was a cause of frustration for Burleigh; it was clear to him that Babe was hired as a sideshow attraction. Babe would belt balls over the Ebbets Field right-field wall in batting practice, but as a first-base coach, Ruth's mind would wander and he would lose concentration.

It soon became clear that Durocher was there as manager-in-waiting. Sure enough, by 1939 Grimes and Ruth were gone and Durocher had taken over as manager.

Maybe picking **Carl Erskine** ahead of some other Dodgers pitchers is a sentimental choice. Carl was, and is, one of my dearest friends and was my roommate with the Dodgers, so perhaps it appears that I'm bending over backward a little for a buddy—until you look at his record. He won 61 percent of his decisions (Editor's note: he had 26 wins in relief and won 59 percent of his starts), pitched two no-hitters, won 20 games in 1953, won two games in the

Carl Erskine gets a congratulatory handshake from vice presidential candidate Senator Richard Nixon after a five-hit victory over the Yankees in Game 5 of the 1952 World Series.

World Series, and had as much guts as any pitcher I've ever seen. You had to know him—to be around him and play behind him every day as I did—to really appreciate him.

Erskine wasn't a big guy, just 5'10" and about 165 pounds, and he pitched his entire career, all 12 years of it, in pain. He hurt his shoulder in his rookie season, and the pain never went away. Imagine what it must be like to hurt every time you throw a pitch. Yet Carl not only gutted it out, he excelled.

Erskine could pitch, and he was smart. He had a great change-up, a great overhand curveball, and he was what we call "sneaky fast." A hitter would be looking for that change or curveball, and Carl would pump the fastball right by him.

Erskine was a big favorite in Brooklyn not only for his great pitching but also for his nickname, Oisk, which came to him from a routine by comedian Phil Foster, a Brooklyn native whose act was predicated on his Brooklyn accent. Foster would do this bit in which he was a typical Dodgers fan rooting for his favorite team. He'd be in the stands, and on the mound was Erskine, or as Foster called him, "Oiskine," and Foster would yell, "Come on, Oisk."

Carl is a classy, elegant, and proper fellow from Indiana, but he has a droll sense of humor. Roy Campanella always used to tell the pitchers, "Don't shake me off. I'm in charge. What I put down, you throw. You do what I tell you, and I'll make you a great pitcher."

Campy kept saying that to Erskine, and one day Carl got beat, 2–1. The next day he cut the box score out of the newspaper, handed it to Campy, and said, "Remember how you kept telling me how you're going to make me a great pitcher? That I should throw what you call for? How come this box score says 'Losing Pitcher Erskine' and not 'Losing Catcher Campanella'?"

Erskine could pitch, and he was smart. He had a great change-up, a great overhand curveball, and he was what we call "sneaky fast." A hitter would be looking for that change or curveball, and Carl would pump the fastball right by him.

In Game 3 of the 1953 World Series against the Yankees, Erskine put on a clinic. He had started Game 1 in Yankee Stadium but was removed after allowing four runs in the first inning. We lost Game 2, and Charlie Dressen brought Erskine back for Game 3 in Ebbets Field after only one day off. But the situation was desperate. We were down two games to none and needed a win badly, and Erskine was the sort of competitor who welcomed the opportunity to avenge what happened in the first game.

Erskine's overhand curveball that day was the best I'd ever seen it. In the bottom of the eighth, Campy hit a home run off Vic Raschi to break a 2–2 tie, and we went to the ninth with a one-run lead. Erskine struck out pinch-hitter Don Bollweg for his 13th strikeout of the game, which tied the World

Series record. Raschi was scheduled to hit next, but Casey Stengel sent up Johnny Mize, the Yankees' pinch-hitter deluxe, to bat for Raschi.

Years later, Mickey Mantle told me that Mize was on the bench watching Erskine strike out all those hitters—he got Mantle four times—and he was saying, "How can you let that guy strike you out?"

Then Mize got up and he struck out. Carl threw his overhand curveball, and Mize swung so hard he almost screwed himself into the ground. His teammates were sitting on the bench laughing, Mantle harder than the rest. It was Erskine's 14th strikeout of the game and the World Series record until Sandy Koufax broke it 10 years later.

Mickey Mantle told me, "Man, I'm glad I didn't get up again because he woulda got me five times. That overhand curve was killing me."

Statistical Summaries

All statistics are from player's Dodgers career only.

PITCHING

G = Games

W = Games won

L = Games lost

PCT = Winning percentage

SHO = Shutouts

SO = Strikeouts

ERA = Earned run average

Right-Handed Pitcher	Years	G	W	L	PCT	SHO	SO	ERA
Don Drysdale *Posted a 1.40 ERA in eight All-Star contests*	1956–69	518	209	166	.557	49	2,486	2.95
Don Newcombe *Stole home against the Pirates on May 26, 1955*	1949–51 1954–58	258	123	66	.651	22	913	3.51

continued	**Years**	**G**	**W**	**L**	**PCT**	**SHO**	**SO**	**ERA**
Dazzy Vance *Struck out the side on nine pitches in the third inning against the Cubs on September 14, 1924*	1922–32 1935	378	190	131	.592	29	1,918	3.17
Burleigh Grimes *Led NL with 11 hit batsmen in 1923*	1918–26	318	158	121	.566	20	952	3.47
Carl Erskine *Second in NL in games started in both 1953 and 1954*	1948–59	335	122	78	.610	14	981	4.00

FIELDING

PO = Putouts

A = Assists

E = Errors

DP = Double plays

TC/G = Total chances divided by games played

FA = Fielding average

Right-Handed Pitcher	**PO**	**A**	**E**	**DP**	**TC/G**	**FA**
Don Drysdale	188	686	59	55	1.8	.937
Don Newcombe	126	254	14	21	1.5	.964
Dazzy Vance	116	535	14	25	1.8	.979
Burleigh Grimes	133	763	47	36	3.0	.950
Carl Erskine	105	262	20	20	1.2	.948

TEN

Left-Handed Pitcher

If you had seen **Sandy Koufax** the first time I saw him, you never would have imagined that he would become what he became—the greatest pitcher I've ever seen and possibly the greatest ever. I never saw Cy Young, Walter Johnson, Lefty Grove, or a lot of other great old-time pitchers, but of those I have seen, nobody was better than Sandy. Every time he went out there, you knew he had a chance to pitch a no-hitter. And he pitched four of them.

Yet when Sandy first came to Brooklyn as a 19-year-old in 1955, he couldn't throw the ball inside the batting cage during batting practice. I wondered how he was on the ballclub. The fact is, he was on the club because the Dodgers had given him a bonus to sign out of the University of Cincinnati, and in those days, any bonus player that received at least $4,000 to sign had to be carried on the major

> 1. SANDY KOUFAX
>
> 2. PREACHER ROE
>
> 3. JOHNNY PODRES
>
> 4. FERNANDO VALENZUELA
>
> 5. TOMMY JOHN

league roster for two full seasons. It was intended to help keep parity in baseball by penalizing teams that were rich enough to stockpile good young players. But watching him, I couldn't help but wonder why they gave him the bonus.

It turns out that they gave Koufax the bonus because he had a great arm. When I first came up, there were so many pitchers, like Nelson Potter and Stu Miller, who couldn't throw hard. They relied on control and trick pitches, such as spitballs, forkballs, knuckleballs, and screwballs, stuff like that. Guys who threw as hard as Sandy were rare back then.

Another reason the Dodgers signed Koufax is that he was a Brooklyn kid, and the Dodgers didn't want to see someone from their own backyard succeed with another team. Ironically, the Brooklyn boy's greatest years came after the Dodgers left Brooklyn.

In his first two years, Sandy won only 4 games and pitched in 28, mostly in relief in one-sided games. He'd start a game occasionally, but he walked almost as many batters as he struck out.

Koufax became a pitcher when he learned, with the help of catcher Norm Sherry, to stop squeezing the ball—to just grip it, relax, and throw it. He became the greatest pitcher I ever saw. The transformation was miraculous. From 1963 to 1966, he put together perhaps the four greatest seasons any pitcher ever had. Look at his numbers:

	W–L	ERA	CG	Innings	K	Shutouts
1963	25–5	1.88	20	311	306	11
1964	19–5	1.74	15	223	223	7
1965	26–8	2.04	27	335⅔	382	8
1966	27–9	1.73	27	323	317	5

It's hard to imagine any pitcher in the history of baseball being more dominant than Koufax was in those four years. When the Dodgers played the Twins in Minnesota in the seventh game of the 1965 World Series, Sandy had had only two days' rest and Don Drysdale three; it was Drysdale's turn to pitch. Walter Alston went up to Don and said, "Don, I know it's your turn to pitch, but Sandy says he's ready."

And Drysdale said, "What the hell are you coming to me for? If I was the manager, I'd pitch Sandy. I'll be ready. I'll go down to the bullpen and I'll be ready if something happens, but I'd pitch him too."

Sandy went out and pitched a three-hit shutout and struck out 10, and the Dodgers won the World Series.

After the 1966 season, Koufax retired. Without a doubt, he could have continued pitching, and winning (look at what he did in his last year), but he retired because of an arthritic left elbow. He had not yet reached his 31st birthday.

Arguably the best pitcher of all time, Sandy Koufax is an easy choice as the Dodgers' top left-hander.

Jim Kaat's major league career spanned three commissioners, four decades, five teams in six cities, seven presidential administrations (from Eisenhower to Reagan), and the entire period of Sandy Koufax's dominance with the Los Angeles Dodgers. Being in different leagues, before interleague play, Kaat would never see Koufax pitch or compete against him, except for one time.

It was the World Series of 1965, Kaat's Minnesota Twins against Koufax's Dodgers.

"The Series opened in Minnesota," Kaat said. "Mudcat Grant got the Game 1 assignment for us against Drysdale, who was pitching instead of Koufax because it was a Jewish holiday. I would draw Koufax in Game 2. Just my luck!

"When I learned that Koufax would miss Game 1 because of Yom Kippur, my first thought was, 'Wow, that's going to be pretty neat, facing Sandy Koufax.'"

The Twins knocked Drysdale out in the third inning and beat the Dodgers, 8–2, to set up the second-game match-up of left-handers, 26-year-old Kaat, who had won 18 games for Minnesota, against 26-game-winner Koufax, the game's premier pitcher. Kaat remembers that day well:

> I had never seen him pitch in person. In fact, the only time I had seen him pitch was in the 1963 World Series. There was only one game of the week in those days, on Saturday afternoon, and when that was on television, we were playing, so I never was able to see the game. [Editor's note: Game of the Week was a television show that broadcast one major league game per week.] I never even saw him pitch in spring training, so this was going to be my first look at him up close.
>
> We were in the bullpen warming up for Game 2, a cold, damp, Minnesota autumn afternoon. The bullpens were right next to each other, and we were so close I could have reached out and touched him. I could hear his ball go "whoosh," while I was throwing my little "pfft." At one point, Koufax looked over at me and said, "You guys don't always play in this weather, do you?"
>
> I thought, "Maybe we've got a chance because we're used to playing in the cold and they're not."

The game started, and we both went three up, three down in the first few innings. I got them out in the third, and I came into the dugout and sat next to Johnny Sain, our pitching coach.

"John," I said, "if I give up a run, this game's over. There's not a man alive can hit this guy."

The game remained scoreless until the bottom of the sixth, when the Twins scored two runs off Koufax on a couple of scratch hits, an error, and a double by Tony Oliva. The Dodgers rallied in the seventh, scored a run, and removed Koufax for a pinch-hitter, but Kaat survived the rally and preserved a 2–1 lead. With Koufax gone, the Twins padded their lead and won the game, 5–1.

Kaat and Koufax met again in Game 5, and this time Koufax was at the top of his game. He pitched a four-hitter, struck out 10, and the Dodgers won, 7–0. When the Twins took Game 6, it set up a third match-up between Kaat and Koufax in Game 7, both pitching on two days' rest.

"Because he was coming back after only two days' rest, Koufax didn't throw many curveballs that day," said Kaat. "He tried to throw a few early in the game, but he wasn't getting them over, so he scrapped the curve and threw nothing but fastballs, one after another, and nobody could touch him. He was so overpowering, I actually felt sorry for our hitters. I batted against him four times in the Series, and it was a joke. He'd throw me that old 'radio ball'—you can hear it, but you can't see it—and the only time I made contact was when I tried to bunt with two strikes and fouled it off. He was awesome."

Koufax stymied the Twins on three hits, struck out 10, and beat Kaat and the Twins, 2–0, to win the World Series. A year later, Koufax retired. He and Kaat would never pitch against each other again, but they would meet occasionally.

"We both live in Florida, and I have run into him at charity golf tournaments," Kaat said. "When the Texas Rangers honored Nolan Ryan, he wanted Koufax there, and Sandy and I were staying at the same hotel. He was a friend of Rangers manager Kevin Kennedy from their Dodgers days, and we sat around Kennedy's office and had a conversation. Later, I hooked up with him at the hotel. But that was the extent of it.

"I wouldn't say we're good friends. I don't see him often, but when I do, he's always cordial and always a gentleman. And he's still the best pitcher I've ever seen."

Koufax always could throw hard. The first thing he had to do to become a winning pitcher was learn to throw strikes, which he did by relaxing his grip and just letting it go instead of trying to throw it as hard as he could. He was throwing hard anyway. And then when Sandy started getting that overhand curveball over the plate consistently, he was practically unhittable.

With the way the game has changed— the emergence of the relief pitcher and pitchers on pitch counts who rarely complete what they start—I feel safe in saying that we will never again see a pitcher like Koufax.

One of the funniest things I ever saw was in 1964 when I was playing for the Giants and Koufax was pitching against Juan Marichal, which was rare. They were two pitchers who pretty much guaranteed their teams a win. Neither would give up many runs, so managers would set up their rotation to make sure they would not pitch against each other.

As usual, Marichal and Koufax were on their games that day, and Marichal kept saying, "How come you can't hit this guy?"

Then it was Marichal's turn to hit; he went up to the plate and Sandy quickly got two strikes on him. Then Koufax threw him that overhand curveball that started head high and then broke down into the dirt. Marichal swung straight down on the pitch and broke his bat on home plate. Marichal came back to the dugout, and we were all sitting on the bench laughing.

"Go ahead and laugh," Marichal said. "Now I know why you can't hit him."

You can name all the great pitchers in baseball history—from Cy Young and Walter Johnson to Roger Clemens and Randy Johnson—and Sandy Koufax will always be on that list. In my book, he's at the top of the list.

With the way the game has changed—the emergence of the relief pitcher and pitchers on pitch counts who rarely complete what they start—I feel safe in saying that we will never again see a pitcher like Koufax.

After the 1947 season, the Dodgers made a trade with the Pirates that turned out to be one of the best trades in the team's history. It started a chain reaction of moves that would help form the team that would win three pennants over six years. In the deal, the Dodgers sent Dixie Walker and two pitchers, Hal Gregg and Vic Lombardi, to Pittsburgh. Walker was a big fan favorite in Brooklyn, a consistent .300 hitter, but he was getting older (37 at the time) and he had asked to be traded because he didn't want to play on the same team with Jackie Robinson.

Preacher Roe gets a hug from team president Branch Rickey after Roe shut down the
Yankees in a 1–0 victory in the second game of the 1949 World Series.

Trading Walker opened up right field, allowing the Dodgers to move Carl
Furillo from center to right. And that opened up center field and gave me my
chance to play regularly. For that alone I am grateful for the trade, but there
were others reasons to be grateful. In return for Walker, Gregg, and Lombardi, the Dodgers got an infielder, Billy Cox, and a left-handed pitcher,
Elwin Charles "Preacher" Roe, so nicknamed because he liked to tell
long-winded stories in his slow, Arkansas twang.

Both Cox and Roe had been underachievers in Pittsburgh. Cox had been
an average shortstop for the Pirates, but the Dodgers got him for third base,
and he became a magician at that position. Roe was something else. In four
seasons with the Pirates, he won 34 games and lost 47, nothing to get excited

about. However, he was pitching for one of the worst teams in baseball, and those of us who hit against him knew he was better than his record.

To look at both of our new players you wouldn't think much of them. They didn't look like ballplayers; they were so scrawny and skinny that you would think they could be knocked over by a stiff Chicago wind or unable to endure the rigors of a 154-game baseball season. Cox was just 29 years old when we got him and Roe was 33, but they both ambled slowly with their shoulders hunched over, so they each appeared to be at least 10 years older than they actually were.

When Preacher came over, he told me, "You cost me my slider. I threw you a slider one time and you hit a double off the scoreboard, and Frisch [Pirates manager Frankie Frisch] wouldn't let me throw it anymore. He took away my slider, then he took away my curveball, and then he took away my change-up. The only thing he left me with was my fastball."

When he came to Brooklyn, Preacher brought his whole arsenal with him, almost all of which were legal pitches. He would load one up once in a while, but only when he needed to. I'm not telling tales. After he retired, Preach wrote a magazine article titled "The Outlawed Spitball Was My Money Pitch."

Preacher was a good guy and a good pitcher who became a *great* pitcher in Brooklyn. He was a pleasure to play behind because he worked quickly and he threw strikes. When a pitcher can do both those things, it keeps his fielders alert and they play better. Preacher always had an idea of what he wanted to do on the mound, and he had such pinpoint control (in his career he pitched almost 2,000 innings and walked only 504 batters) that he could throw the ball where he wanted and knew where the batters would hit it, so he would move his outfielders according to where he would be pitching.

Roe gave up a lot of home runs, but like a lot of good pitchers, most of them came with the bases empty. He would pitch to the scoreboard. If he had, say, a four-run lead, he'd let the batter hit the ball rather than walk him.

One time, he gave up five home runs, each with the bases empty, and won the game, 7–5. After he gave up his fifth homer in that game, a blast into the upper deck in center field, and the umpire had thrown him a new ball, Preach turned around, walked toward second base rubbing up the baseball, and shouted to me, "Hey, Duke. Play a little higher."

We liked to get on Roe for his hitting, or lack thereof. He had a career batting average of .110. When he got a hit, we would pretend to fall down in shock. Late in his career, in 1953, Preacher swung, made contact, and wonder of wonders, the ball flew out of the park. We couldn't believe it and, apparently, neither could Preacher. After he hit the ball, he just stood at home plate, not knowing what to do next. Finally, he began trotting toward first base. We all got on him about it, even Jake Pitler, our first-base coach, did.

"How should I know where to go?" Preach shouted as he trotted to first. "I never hit one of these things before."

In his seven seasons in Brooklyn, Roe won 93 games and lost only 37. In 1950–1951 he was 41–14. And in 1951 he was 22–3 and walked only 64 batters in 257⅔ innings.

Years later, at a fantasy camp, someone asked him, "What was your greatest accomplishment in 1951?"

He replied, "I weighed 150 pounds, I was 6'2", I was built like a pencil, I pitched in 100-degree weather, and I pitched 19 complete games. That was my biggest accomplishment. Complete games."

There is no bigger hero in Brooklyn baseball, no player more celebrated, than **Johnny Podres**—all because of one game. Not that John didn't win other games for the Dodgers—41 in Brooklyn and 95 in Los Angeles—but that one game made him a legend in Brooklyn. He's the only pitcher in the history of Brooklyn baseball to win the clinching game of a World Series title.

Podres was one of the best money pitchers I've ever seen. If we needed to win a game, besides Koufax, John's the guy we'd give the ball to. And we needed to win Game 7 of the 1955 World Series against the Yankees. Podres had had only a mediocre season, 9–10, but he won Game 3 when we needed it (we were behind, two games to none, and John pitched a complete game, 8–3 victory), and Walter Alston gave him the ball for Game 7.

There are two things I always knew about John: he would come up big in big games, and he would never be scared. He was only 23 years old at the time, and he was as cocky as they come. The day before the game he said, "Just get me one run and we'll win tomorrow. I'll shut 'em out."

We got him two runs that day, one more than he needed. Gil Hodges singled home Roy Campanella in the fourth and hit a sacrifice fly in the sixth, and Sandy Amoros made a tremendous catch to rob Yogi Berra of an RBI double in the sixth. That's all Podres needed. True to his word, he shut out the Yankees. He allowed eight hits but kept pitching out of trouble and stranded eight runners, and we won, 2–0, Brooklyn's only world championship.

Podres had some good years in L.A., winning 13 games or more for six straight years. His best season was 1961, when he was 18–5. Podres' career winning percentage was .561, but his winning percentage in the World Series was .800 (4–1). His career earned run average was 3.67, but his ERA in the World Series was 2.11.

After he retired, John became an outstanding pitching coach for the Twins and the Phillies. Podres knows the game exceptionally well. In Minnesota he

Johnny Podres' full motion is captured in this photo sequence from his historic Game 7 victory to clinch the 1955 World Series.

had Frank Viola, who became a 24-game winner and a Cy Young Award winner, and in Philadelphia he helped Curt Schilling become the great pitcher he
is today.

But for all his accomplishments, Johnny Podres' legacy will always be his
win one October afternoon in Yankee Stadium in 1955.

What can I say about **Fernando Valenzuela**? He was a barrel-chested kid,
the youngest of 12 children from a poor Mexican farming family. The
Dodgers tried for a long time to sign him because they knew he would be a
huge gate attraction for Los Angeles' large Mexican population. At the same
time, they got an outstanding pitcher, but I wonder if the Dodgers ever
dreamed he would be as good as he was.

Fernando Valenzuela
pitches in the 1986
All-Star Game in
Houston, where he
tied Carl Hubbell's
mark of five
consecutive strikeouts.

Fernando took Los Angeles by storm. Whenever he pitched in Dodger Stadium there was a full house. It became known as Fernandomania. People swam across the Mexican border to get up there to see him pitch. And for a few years, he was as good as anybody.

He threw a hellacious screwball that reminded old-timers of the great Giants Hall of Famer left-hander Carl Hubbell, and he had that funky delivery where he would look up to the heavens before delivering the ball, which was a great weapon to confuse hitters. He won 141 games for the Dodgers in 11 seasons and was one of the most dominant pitchers in baseball in the eighties.

Whenever he pitched in Dodger Stadium there was a full house. It became known as Fernandomania. People swam across the Mexican border to get up there to see him pitch.

Fernando was an immediate sensation for the Dodgers, winning his first 10 major league decisions. He had appeared in 10 games in 1980 and hadn't allowed an earned run, so, officially, he was still a rookie in 1981. That was the strike-shortened season, but Valenzuela was 13–7 and led the league in games started (25), complete games (11), innings pitched (192), strikeouts (180), and shutouts (8). He pitched five shutouts in his first eight starts, and his eight shutouts tied the rookie record in a season that was shortened by one-third because of the strike. He won both the Rookie of the Year and Cy Young awards. He was the first rookie ever to win the Cy Young Award.

He won 21 games in 1986 and led the league in complete games two more times. Despite his dumpy physique, Fernando was a good athlete who won a Gold Glove and a Silver Bat, which goes to the top hitter at his position. He also played the outfield once when the Dodgers ran out of position players in a 21-inning game.

Comparisons between Carl Hubbell and Valenzuela were evoked even more during in the 1986 All-Star Game. Hubbell provided one of the great moments in baseball history in the 1934 All-Star Game in the Polo Grounds when he struck out, in succession, Babe Ruth, Lou Gehrig, Jimmie Foxx, Al Simmons, and Joe Cronin, all future Hall of Famers. Fifty-three years later, in Houston, Fernando matched Hubbell by striking out, in succession, Don Mattingly, Cal Ripken Jr., Jesse Barfield, Lou Whitaker, and Ted Higuera.

Tommy John would rate higher than fifth on my list of left-handed pitchers, but he was a Dodger for only 87 of his 277 major league wins and only one of his three 20-win seasons.

Tommy was what hitters call a comfortable pitcher. He was comfortable to hit off. By that I mean he wasn't the type of pitcher who would overpower the hitter with his fastball or intimidate him with a vigorous delivery, as guys like Randy Johnson (known as the Big Unit) does and John Candelaria used to do. Pitchers like them make the hitter uncomfortable at the plate.

Tommy was a comfortable at-bat, but hitters couldn't center the ball against him. He'd sink it and move it around—on the corners, just off the corners. Hitters would come up with weak ground balls or soft pop flies, and they'd go back to the bench shaking their heads; they couldn't wait to get up there again. They were sure they'd get him the next time, but they rarely did.

Tommy had great control, and he changed speeds well. He'd just baffle hitters, keep them off balance, and get them out.

It's ironic, and unfair in a way, that for all he accomplished as a pitcher—the 288 wins, the three 20-win seasons, the 6–2 record in the playoffs and World Series, and the 26-year career that spanned seven presidents—Tommy is probably best known for surgery to transplant a tendon into his pitching arm. Dr. Frank Jobe, the great surgeon who worked for the Dodgers, performed the procedure on John in 1974. Dr. Jobe took a tendon from Tommy's right arm and transplanted it into his left elbow.

Tommy was the first to have that surgery. Now, about one out of every three pitchers has had that same operation, and it has saved many careers. The procedure has come to be known as "Tommy John surgery," and, sadly, a lot of today's young pitchers think Tommy John was a doctor, not a major league pitcher.

Tommy, who has a great sense of humor, has said that before he went into surgery, he told Dr. Jobe to "put in a Koufax fastball."

"He did," Tommy jokes, "but it was Mrs. Koufax's."

Tommy John (foreground) and Steve Garvey celebrate the final out of John's complete-game victory over the Philadelphia Phillies to clinch the National League pennant on October 8, 1977. *Photo courtesy of Bettmann/Corbis.*

Statistical Summaries

All statistics are from player's Dodgers career only.

PITCHING

G = Games
W = Games won
L = Games lost
PCT = Winning percentage
SHO = Shutouts
SO = Strikeouts
ERA = Earned run average

Left-Handed Pitcher	Years	G	W	L	PCT	SHO	SO	ERA
Sandy Koufax *Pitched 10 complete-game 1–0 victories during his career*	1955–66	397	165	87	.655	40	2,396	2.76
Preacher Roe *Completed all three of his World Series starts*	1948–54	201	93	37	.715	12	632	3.26
Johnny Podres *Fanned eight straight Philadelphia batters July 1, 1962*	1953–55 1956	366	136	104	.567	23	1,331	3.66

continued	Years	G	W	L	PCT	SHO	SO	ERA
Fernando Valenzuela *Won the only Gold Glove of his career in 1986*	1980–90	331	141	116	.549	29	1,759	3.31
Tommy John *Career 4–1 NLCS record with 2.08 ERA*	1972–74 1976–78	182	87	42	.675	11	649	2.97

FIELDING

PO = Putouts

A = Assists

E = Errors

DP = Double plays

TC/G = Total chances divided by games played

FA = Fielding average

Left-Handed Pitcher	PO	A	E	DP	TC/G	FA
Sandy Koufax	64	228	14	13	0.8	.954
Preacher Roe	53	195	6	20	1.3	.976
Johnny Podres	69	283	17	22	1.0	.954
Fernando Valenzuela	164	451	23	28	1.9	.964
Tommy John	46	270	7	20	1.8	.976

ELEVEN

Relief Pitcher

I played in an era when relief pitchers generally were older guys, veterans who could no longer pitch nine innings or guys with a trick pitch, like a screwball, forkball, knuckleball, or—do I dare say it?—spitball.

Pitchers usually finished what they started in my day. Twenty and thirty years ago, relief pitchers (they weren't called closers in those days) would come in when the game was on the line and there were runners on base, and they often would pitch two, three, or more innings. That's the reason they didn't put up the saves numbers that you see today. It's not that they couldn't; they simply were used differently.

That all seemed to change when saves became an official statistic. Saves

1. Eric Gagne

2. Clem Labine

3. Ron Perranoski

4. Hugh Casey

5. Ed Roebuck

weren't recorded back in the day; when you see the number of saves listed next to a pitcher from the fifties and earlier, those were added later by statisticians who scoured box scores and determined the number of saves years after the fact.

Since saves became an official statistic, relief pitchers have risen in importance, and today they are among the highest-paid players in the game. These days they come into a game to start an inning, often with a three-run lead. In my day relievers usually came in when trouble was brewing, with runners on base and the game on the line. That's not how they do it today, and that's what separates the old-time reliever from the modern closer. Today's relievers are not necessarily better than guys like Hugh Casey, Elroy Face, Stu Miller, Hoyt Wilhelm, and Clem Labine; they just operate under a different system. Another thing that's changed is that in my day most relief pitchers were starters early in their careers. Today, kids are groomed to be relief pitchers as early as high school.

But these differences in the game take nothing away from **Eric Gagne**, who would have been a standout in any era. It's just that if he had pitched 30 years ago, his role would have been different. Gagne, who is from Canada, actually came to the Dodgers as a starting pitcher, but in his first three seasons he had records of 1–1, 4–6, and 6–7. Not very dominant. He didn't have the variety of pitches a starter needs to be successful. But he threw hard and could be overpowering for an inning or two. So the Dodgers turned him into a reliever, and he became a great one.

In 2002, his first season closing games for the Dodgers, he was 4–1, had a team-record 52 saves, and had an earned-run average of 1.97. In 77 games he pitched 82⅓ innings (barely an inning per outing), allowed only 55 hits (a little more than a half-hit per game), and struck out 114 batters (1⅓ strikeouts per inning and 12½ strikeouts per nine innings).

The following year he was even better. Although his record was 2–3, he increased his team record to 55 saves and had an ERA of 1.20. Again, he appeared in 77 games and pitched 82⅓ innings, the same as the previous year. This time he allowed only 34 hits (that's a phenomenal .4 hits per inning), struck out 137 batters (1.6 strikeouts per game and 15 strikeouts per nine innings), and was named National League Cy Young Award winner.

Gagne slipped a little in 2004, but his numbers were still awesome. He was 2–3 with a 2.19 earned run average and had 45 saves. He appeared in 70 games and for the third straight year pitched exactly 82⅓ innings, with 53 hits and 114 strikeouts.

In his first three years as the Dodgers' closer, Gagne has saved 152 games and set a major league record by converting an incredible 84 consecutive save opportunities.

Eric Gagne works on his 55th save of the 2003 season on September 25 in San Diego.

A perfect example of the difference between relievers then and now is **Clem Labine**. Clem was the Dodgers' best reliever in the fifties and one of the top two or three relievers in all of baseball at the time. But that fact is not supported by his stats, at least not when you compare them to the numbers compiled by today's relievers.

For example, in his best years, from 1955 to 1958, Labine had only 61 saves. Today's top closers get almost that many in one season. But Clem also won 34 games in those four years, and he started 13 games. It also should be pointed out that in those four years, the Dodgers' pitching staff had 166 complete games, so the opportunity for saves was not as great as it is today.

Clem came to the Dodgers as a starter. He started the second game of the three-game playoff against the Giants in 1951, and he pitched a complete-game shutout to force that infernal sudden-death third game, the one in which, it pains me to remember, Bobby Thomson hit his famous home run.

Labine had great promise as a starter, but he also was earning the reputation of a guy who could come in and shut down the opposition when the game was on the line. So more and more they began to use him late in the game in relief.

Labine had great promise as a starter, but he also was earning the reputation of a guy who could come in and shut down the opposition when the game was on the line. So more and more they began to use him late in the game in relief. At the time, relief pitching was getting to be more important because starters, for the most part, were completing fewer games. Clem had a great sinker that enabled him to get double plays and that made him a good guy to bring in with a game on the line and runners on base.

Labine also endeared himself to Dodgers fans with his handling of the great Stan Musial. "Stan the Man" was a notorious Dodger-killer and Brooklyn's most feared opponent. But Labine retired him a remarkable 49 consecutive times.

In 1956 Labine led the league in saves, with 19. The next year he led the league again with 17 saves. But hardly anybody noticed because they weren't paying attention to saves in those days. Nobody even talked about saves then. It was not an official statistic, and they weren't printed in the newspaper.

As a sign of the times, in the 1955 World Series against the Yankees—the only World Series the Dodgers ever won in Brooklyn—Clem won Game 4 by pitching the last four and two-thirds innings in relief, and then he came back the next day and pitched the final three innings to save Game 5. You won't see today's closers do that, or this. In 1956, in addition to his league-leading 19

One of Clem Labine's claims to fame was that he had Stan Musial's number; Labine retired the Hall of Famer a remarkable 49 consecutive times. *Photo courtesy of Diamond Images/Getty Images.*

saves, Labine won 10 games and made three starts. He pitched two innings in relief in Game 3 of the World Series against the Yankees, and then, after Don Larsen's perfect game in Game 5, which put us down three games to two, Walter Alston, strapped for starters, gave the ball to Labine to start Game 6. Clem pitched a complete-game, 10-inning shutout and beat the Yankees, 1–0, to force Game 7.

To me, the addition of **Ron Perranoski** to the Dodgers just before the start of the 1960 season was a blessing and a curse. It was a curse because he came in a trade that sent Don Zimmer, one of my oldest and dearest friends, to the Cubs. But it was a blessing because we got a great relief pitcher that I soon came to appreciate as a teammate and a friend.

Pitcher Ron Perranoski (right) looks out to the bullpen during a tight spot in the 1966 World Series at Dodger Stadium. *Photo courtesy of Focus on Sport/Getty Images.*

168

Perranoski was at the vanguard of the relief pitcher's emerging prominence. He had been a starting pitcher in the minor leagues, but the Dodgers sent him to the bullpen and initially used him as a left-handed specialist against left-handed hitters. By 1962 he was the Dodgers' stopper. He led the league with 70 appearances, won 6 games, and saved 20 others. The following year he won 16 games, all in relief, and saved 21.

Ron spent seven seasons with the Dodgers, who traded him to Minnesota after the 1967 season. When he left the Dodgers, Perranoski was the team's career leader in saves, with 101, a record that has since been passed, as times changed, by Jim Brewer, Jeff Shaw, Todd Worrell, and Eric Gagne.

Looking back, I think the Dodgers traded him prematurely. Once he got acclimated to relief pitching, he became one of the top relievers in the American League. He led the AL in saves in 1969 with 31, and in 1970 with 34.

After he retired, Perranoski came back to the Dodgers and was an outstanding pitching coach for 14 years. He coached a staff that won two World Series and was instrumental in the development of Fernando Valenzuela, Orel Hershiser, and Bob Welch.

*I*n his 60-plus years in baseball as player, coach, scout, manager, and general manager, Clyde King has seen all the wide, sweeping changes to the game: from two eight-team leagues to expansion, from a nine-man game to the designated hitter, from the reserve clause to free agency. He has seen the arrival of the wild-card, interleague play, computer printouts, radar guns, and pitch counts.

"I remember a time when pitchers pitched doubleheaders," King said, "or pitched a complete game one day and then came back two days later and pitched in relief. I remember when there were four-man rotations and pitchers finished what they started. Today, you rarely see a starting pitcher finish a game. If a starter goes six or seven innings, the manager will take him out and go to his bullpen.

"When I managed the Giants, if I tried to get Gaylord Perry or Juan Marichal out of the game in the seventh inning, I'd have to go to the mound with a shotgun."

Of all the changes King has seen in his 60-plus years, none has had as big an impact on the field as the emergence of the relief pitcher, or closer, a role King filled effectively, but without fanfare, for the Brooklyn Dodgers in 1951.

When King arrived in Brooklyn in 1944, the team's star reliever, Hugh Casey, was fulfilling his military commitment. Two years later Casey returned to assume his role as the dominant reliever of his time.

"Casey was a chubby guy . . . barrel-chested," remembered King, "and he was as tough as nails. He was tough on the mound and tough in the clubhouse. He was the kind of guy if one of his teammates didn't hustle, Casey would chew him out in no uncertain terms.

"On the mound he threw a heavy ball, and he'd knock a hitter down as soon as look at him. He was like Mariano Rivera is today. By that I mean, when Casey came into a game, it usually meant the game was over."

In his heyday—the two years preceding and the two years following World War II—Casey led the National League in relief wins three times and in saves twice. In those four seasons, he saved 43 games. That's 43 saves total, not

169

an average of 43 per year. Today, the game's better closers save more than 43 games per year.

Saves didn't become an official statistic until 1969, after which research- ers and statisticians pored over old box scores to update the save records of all pitchers who toiled in the "presave era."

"Back then," said King, "we didn't even know what a save was, and most of Casey's wins and saves came in games in which he would enter in the eighth inning, or the seventh, or even the sixth. That's the big difference between the relievers of my day and the closers of today. If Casey were pitching today, used the way today's closers are used, I have no doubt he would save 40 or 50 games a season."

King himself led the league with 13 relief wins in 1951 and was fifth in the league in saves with six. He also started three games and pitched 121⅓ innings in 48 appearances.

King remembers one game in 1947 when he started for the Dodgers against the Pirates. "I pitched against Mel Queen and got beat," he said, laughing. "That was one time the queen trumped the king."

One of the earliest relief specialists was **Hugh Casey**, who came to the Dodgers in 1939 and left after 1948, my second season with the Dodgers. Early in his career, Casey doubled as a starter and a reliever. His best years were taken away from him, though, when he served three years in the mil- itary during World War II. When he returned, he was in his thirties and no longer able to pitch effectively for nine innings, so he became a relief pitcher exclusively. He led the National League in relief wins three times and in saves twice, but to do so with the number of saves he had (13 in 1942 and 18 in 1947) shows that he pitched in a much different era.

Casey was a fierce competitor, a loner, and a tough guy. When I got to the Dodgers, I heard stories about how one spring, when the Dodgers trained in Cuba, he became friendly with the great writer Ernest Hemingway. One night he was invited to Hemingway's house, and he wound up putting on boxing gloves and exchanging punches with "Papa."

Today Casey is best remembered as the guy who threw the famous pitch that Tommy Henrich swung at and missed and Mickey Owen then dropped in Game 4 of the 1941 World Series. It was the ninth inning, the Yankees led

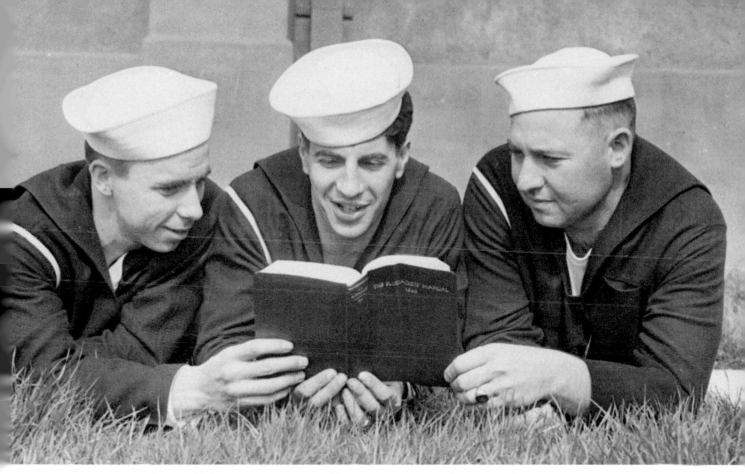

Hugh Casey (right) lost three years to military service during World War II and was more suited to the bullpen upon his return. Here he is shown with Pee Wee Reese (left) and Phil Rizzuto at the navy base in Norfolk, Virginia, in 1943.

the Series two games to one, there were two outs and nobody on base, and the Dodgers were in front, 4–3. The count went to 3–2, so the Dodgers were one strike away from tying the Series.

Casey, who had come into the game in the fifth inning and had held the Yankees scoreless, threw the pitch. Henrich swung and missed, but the ball got past Owen and went to the backstop and Henrich reached first. Then Joe DiMaggio singled, Charlie Keller doubled, Bill Dickey walked, and Joe Gordon doubled. The Yanks scored four runs and won the game, 7–4. The Yankees then won Game 5 and the World Series.

For years, I heard that the pitch Casey threw was a spitball, but that has never been confirmed. Casey never admitted it—but he never denied it either.

Ed Roebuck loosens up before a World Series game against the Yankees in 1955. *Photo courtesy of Diamond Images/Getty Images.*

Ed Roebuck, my teammate with the Dodgers in Brooklyn and Los Angeles, was one of the first pitchers to be what is now known as a set-up man—the guy who comes in to hold the game for the closer. He and Clem Labine were a team, one complementing the other.

Although he wasn't used as set-up men are today, Roebuck often preceded Clem Labine in a game and sometimes was the closer when Clem wasn't available. He spent seven and a half seasons with the Dodgers, won 40 games in relief, and saved 43.

Roebuck would have had an even better career, but he suffered a shoulder injury, which caused him to miss all of the Dodgers' 1959 pennant-winning season. But he was a dedicated and hard worker, and he went through rehabilitation to get himself ready to pitch in 1960, when he won eight games and saved eight more. Two years later, he won ten games, all in relief, and saved nine.

It's funny, but the one thing about Ed that stands out in my mind is a game in 1957 when he came to bat twice in an inning and struck out both times. You can be sure his teammates gave it to him good about that, and we certainly never let him forget it.

I should make mention here of other Dodgers relief pitchers, like Jim Hughes; Joe Black, who had one great season—his rookie year; Phil Regan, "the Vulture"; Steve Howe; Tom Niedenfuer; and the "Iron Man," Mike Marshall.

Marshall was a Dodger for only two and a half seasons, but what he did in one of those years, 1974, was truly remarkable for a relief pitcher. He appeared in a major league–record 106 games (that's an amazing 65 percent of his team's games), pitched 208 innings, won 15 games, saved 21, and was voted the National League Cy Young Award winner.

Statistical Summaries

All statistics are from player's Dodgers career only.

PITCHING

G = Games
W = Games won
L = Games lost
PCT = Winning percentage
SV = Saves
SO = Strikeouts
ERA = Earned run average

Relief Pitcher	Years	G	W	L	PCT	SV	SO	ERA
Eric Gagne *Stranded all 18 inherited runners in 2004*	1999–2005	296	25	21	.543	160	626	3.28
Clem Labine *Had three hits in 1955—all home runs*	1950–60	425	70	52	.574	85	260	3.63
Ron Perranoski *Pitched more than 100 innings five of his first seven seasons*	1961–67 1972	457	54	41	.568	101	461	2.56

continued	Years	G	W	L	PCT	SV	SO	ERA
Hugh Casey *Went 2–0 in 1947 World Series with 0.87 ERA*	1939–42 1946–48	293	70	41	.631	50	325	3.34
Ed Roebuck *Posted a 1.42 ERA in four World Series games*	1955–58 1960–63	322	40	22	.645	43	376	3.46

FIELDING

PO = Putouts

A = Assists

E = Errors

DP = Double plays

TC/G = Total chances divided by games played

FA = Fielding average

Relief Pitcher	PO	A	E	DP	TC/G	FA
Eric Gagne	32	49	1	3	0.3	.988
Clem Labine	81	184	12	14	0.7	.957
Ron Perranoski	36	156	12	10	0.5	.941
Hugh Casey	50	204	6	21	0.9	.977
Ed Roebuck	43	131	10	8	0.6	.946

TWELVE

Manager

Based on their records alone, **Charlie Dressen** isn't in the same class as Walter Alston and Leo Durocher as a manager. Alston and Durocher are in the Hall of Fame, and Dressen isn't. But I played for all three managers—plus a few others—and Dressen is the best manager I ever played for.

Charlie managed the Dodgers in Brooklyn for only three years, 1951, 1952, and 1953, and won 298 games. He won pennants in 1952 and 1953, and in his other year, we finished in a tie with the Giants and lost the three-game playoff. I'll get to why Charlie didn't manage the Dodgers for longer than three years later.

After a mediocre career as a third baseman for the Cincinnati Reds, Dressen managed the Reds for four seasons without much success. In those four seasons, he finished fifth once, sixth once, and eighth twice in an eight-team league

1. CHARLIE DRESSEN

2. WALTER ALSTON

3. LEO DUROCHER

4. TOMMY LASORDA

5. WILBERT ROBINSON

Charlie was let go by Cincinnati, and when Durocher took over as manager of the Dodgers in 1939, he brought Dressen in as a coach. Charlie was a coach for the Dodgers from 1939 to 1950, and we all thought he should have been named manager of the Dodgers in 1947, when Durocher was suspended.

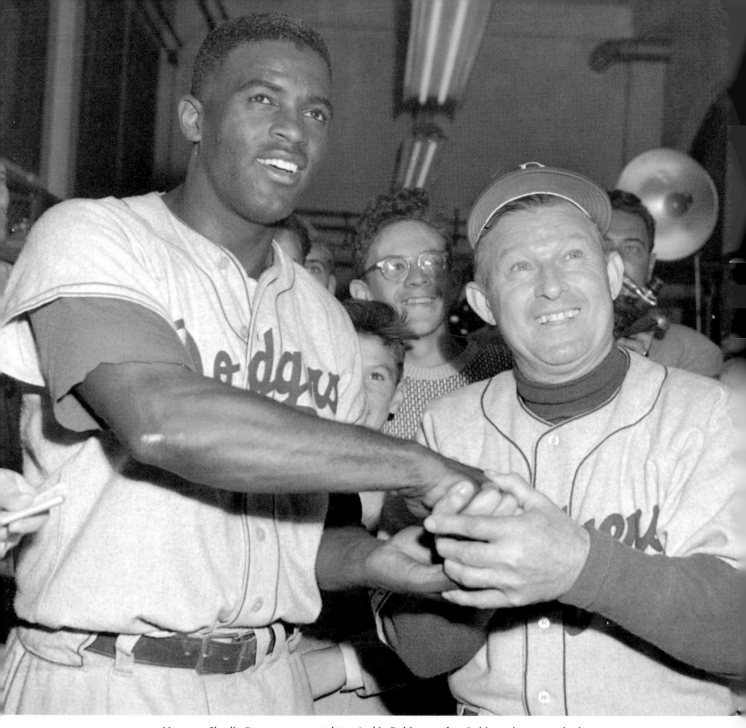

Manager Charlie Dressen congratulates Jackie Robinson after Robinson's game-winning home run in the fourteenth inning beat the Phillies at Shibe Park on September 30, 1951.

Instead, Dressen was passed over, and the job went to Burt Shotton, who managed the game in street clothes.

I always thought that was odd and that it detracted from the manager's control of the game. Connie Mack had done the same thing for 50 years, but he was part-owner of the team he managed, the Philadelphia Athletics. Because he didn't wear a uniform, Shotton was not permitted to go onto the playing field to coach (most managers coached third base in my day), give advice, or change a pitcher. I think it's important for a manager to be in uniform and be part of the team.

Dressen remained as a coach under Shotton, and then he replaced Shotton as manager in 1951. I think Dressen was the most knowledgeable manager that I played for. He knew the game exceptionally well, and he knew how to handle each individual player. He was particularly hard on me, trying to get me to lay off my high fastball, which was out of the strike zone. But I came to understand that it was all for my own good.

Charlie had a problem with the word *I*. He knew the game, and he made sure to let others know that he knew the game. He was great at stealing the opposition's signs, and he used to tell us in team meetings before a big series, "Just hang close 'til the seventh inning, and I'll think of something."

He thought of something one afternoon game in Ebbets Field when he was thrown out of the game in the third inning. Charlie went into the clubhouse and an inning later, I noticed a guy dressed like a member of the ground crew standing in the dugout. I thought I knew all the guys on the ground crew, but this one I didn't recognize. He was wearing those fake glasses with a big nose attached to them and a thick, black mustache. It was Dressen. He spent the rest of the game in the dugout, dressed as a member of the ground crew, and he managed the game from there. Amazingly, the umpires never caught on.

One time before a game with the Giants, while the lineup cards were being exchanged, Walker Cooper, the Giants catcher, represented Leo Durocher at the meeting with the umpires. Cooper took not only the lineup card to home plate, but also a book that he handed to Charlie. The cover of the book said, *What I Know About Baseball* by Charlie Dressen. When Dressen opened the book, he found the word *I* written on every page. Even Charlie was laughing when he came back to our dugout.

179

Durocher and Dressen, when they were together, made an odd couple. I don't think they liked each other. Theirs was kind of a false friendship, if they had any at all. In public they were cordial with each other. I think they respected one another's baseball knowledge, but I also believe there was a lot of envy between them. There had to be a clash of egos because each one thought he was the smartest man in the game. Charlie used to say, "I taught Leo everything he knows about baseball."

When we played the Giants, the game became more a battle of wits between Dressen and Durocher than a game of skill between the players. It was as if both managers were more interested in outsmarting the other than they were in the final score. My recollection is that Charlie had the upper hand on Durocher more times than not, and he took great delight in outwitting his adversary.

There was one time, however, that Leo got the best of Charlie, and it might have been the biggest game they ever managed against each other. I'm referring to the third game of the playoff between the Dodgers and Giants in 1951.

We went to the bottom of the ninth leading 4–1, three outs from the pennant with Don Newcombe sailing along. In case Newk got into trouble, Dressen had Ralph Branca and Carl Erskine warming up in the bullpen. When it came time to replace Newk, Charlie called down to the bullpen and asked coach Clyde Sukeforth which pitcher was throwing better, Branca or Erskine.

"Erskine's bouncing his curveball," Sukey reported.

"OK," Charlie said. "Give me Branca."

You know the rest: Bobby Thomson hit a three-run homer, and the Giants beat us, 5–4. Erskine has said that the pitch he bounced was "the best curveball I ever threw."

Dressen took a lot of criticism for not being decisive and for allowing Sukeforth to dictate which pitcher should come in rather than taking the responsibility of making the decision himself. Despite that one incident, I still think Dressen was an outstanding baseball man. He ran the game very well. He knew how to get to me, and get the best out of me. He'd wake me up. Charlie was a good baseball man and a good guy. He'd get under a player's skin, and he'd aggravate people. He even did the impossible by getting Pee Wee Reese mad at him—Pee Wee never got mad at anything or anybody—by pinch hitting for him.

Basically, Dressen was a good man. He loved to cook, and he'd bring in chili and crab fingers and other stuff that he cooked up in his office.

After Dressen won his second straight pennant, in 1953, he asked Dodgers owner Walter O'Malley for a multiyear contract, which was against team policy. (The story making the rounds at the time was that Charlie was prodded by his wife to ask for a long-term contract.) Neither side would budge, so the Dodgers cut ties with Dressen and replaced him with a longtime minor league manager in their farm system, a relative unknown. His name was Walter Alston.

On November 24, 1953, after the Dodgers had refused to knuckle under to Charlie Dressen's demands for a multiyear contract, they announced that their new manager would be **Walter Alston**. The next day, the *New York Daily News* reported the event with this headline: Walter Who?

Manager Walter Alston (left) and coach Charlie Dressen celebrate the Dodgers' 9–3 win over the White Sox in Game 6 to clinch the 1959 World Series.

In his 60 years as a baseball executive, Emil J. "Buzzie" Bavasi has done it all and seen it all, from celebration, to integration, to migration. As the general manager and architect of the only major league baseball team representing Brooklyn to win a world championship, in 1955, he celebrated. He was running the Dodgers' Nashua farm team in the Class B Eastern League when Branch Rickey sent him two young players: Don Newcombe, a 19-year-old right-handed pitcher, and Roy Campanella, a 24-year-old veteran of the Negro Leagues—thus beginning integration. And he was the Dodgers GM in 1958 when Walter O'Malley pulled up stakes and moved the team to Los Angeles, a cross-country migration.

For all these notable accomplishments, Bavasi's greatest legacy to baseball may be that he recommended, campaigned for, and was instrumental in bringing to Brooklyn as manager an unknown named Walter Alston.

In 1946 Bavasi was handpicked by Dodgers president Branch Rickey to operate the team's minor league affiliate in Nashua, and Bavasi, in turn, had to persuade Alston to remain as the club's player/manager. At the time, Alston, an alumnus of Miami University (Ohio), the renowned "college of coaches," was eager to return to his native Ohio to resume the post-baseball career he had charted for himself, that of a high school teacher and coach.

The tandem of Bavasi and Alston was, according to Newcombe, a fortuitous one in terms of baseball's most noble experiment. "If it weren't for Buzzie Bavasi, I'd have had nothing in baseball," said Newcombe. "Without Mr. Bavasi, Mr. Rickey, and Walter Alston, Roy and I never would have gotten to where we were. I owe everything to them. I've thought about this for 50 years. Suppose Buzzie Bavasi was a bigot, and suppose Walter Alston was a bigot. Our whole lives would be different."

In 1948 Bavasi was named general manager of Montreal, the Dodgers' Triple A team in the International League, and Alston went along with him as manager. On November 28, 1950, Rickey resigned as president of the Dodgers and was succeeded by Walter O'Malley, who summoned Bavasi to Brooklyn to take over the position of general manager.

"After the 1953 season," Bavasi recalled, "Charlie Dressen's wife, Ruth, insisted on a three-year contract with an additional $10,000 per year tax-free expense account. No chance. I felt sorry for Charlie because he would have been satisfied with a one-year deal."

Several names surfaced as possible successors to Dressen, including Pee Wee Reese, Clyde Sukeforth, and Clay Hopper, a successful Triple A manager in the Dodgers' farm system. But Bavasi had another idea.

"Alston was my first and only choice," he said. "O'Malley did not know him, but Fresco Thompson [head of the Dodgers' farm system] and the rest of the minor league people agreed that Walter was the right choice."

It was not, however, a popular choice with fans and the veteran players Alston would have to lead. They were dubious about a man who had no track record and no pedigree and whose only major league experience had been one at-bat with the Cardinals. No Dodgers veteran was more outspoken than the team's most visible and most symbolic player, Jackie Robinson.

Bavasi recalls Robinson's reaction to Alston:

> It's true that in the early years, Jackie and Alston were not on the best of terms. Jackie was of the opinion that Alston, with no major league experience, was not the man for the job. He said things that would have been better left unsaid.
>
> It came to a head on the way north from Vero Beach. We had a game scheduled in Louisville, Pee Wee Reese's hometown. Jackie made some remark to the press that finally got under Walter's skin.
>
> Pee Wee called me and said there could be trouble and it would not be Alston's fault. I told Pee Wee that I thought Walter could handle himself. I later learned that Walter called Jackie into the manager's office and Walter locked the door and said, "Jackie, this has gone far enough. I expect an apology from you or else only one of us is going out this door."
>
> Apparently, Jackie admitted he had gone too far, and he apologized to Walter. From that day on, they never had another problem. In fact, Walter became one of Jackie's biggest boosters.
>
> In my opinion, Alston had all the necessities for a major league manager. He came up through the minor leagues and knew the way the game should be played. His forte was his knowledge of pitching. I credit him with making a pitcher of Sandy Koufax.

Sandy was a local boy, and Alston didn't want to pitch him in Brooklyn because Sandy wasn't ready. He was too wild. He just couldn't come close to home plate, and Alston didn't want to pitch him in front of the home folks. He got to California and Alston still didn't pitch him in 1958. Sandy wanted to quit. I had a talk with him and I talked him out of quitting, but Alston was the only one who had faith in Koufax. Everybody else thought we made a mistake signing him. I didn't have an opinion because I hadn't seen Sandy pitch before he signed.

If it hadn't been for Walter Alston, Sandy Koufax might not have made it in the major leagues. Alston and his pitching coach Joe Becker deserve all the credit in the world for their patience with Koufax, who became the greatest pitcher I ever saw.

As a manager, Alston seemed to always make his moves before the damage took place. His only barometer on whether or not a manager was doing a good job was his record in one-run games. [If he won more one-run games than he lost, it] meant the manager was doing his job.

Walter never overmanaged; he let the players do their job, and he made good use of his coaching staff. After the 1962 season, when we lost to the Giants in a playoff, Leo Durocher, who was Alston's third-base coach, popped off to the press that if he had been the manager we would have won the pennant. Coincidentally, that night I had dinner with Vince Scully at the Friars Club, and we ran into Durocher. I fired him on the spot. The next morning I told Alston that I had fired Leo, and Walter begged me to keep him on. He said he liked having Durocher around and that Leo needed the job. So Durocher retained his job, thanks to Alston.

In addition to his vast knowledge of the game, and his compassion, Alston was a man of great inner strength and a physical presence. According to Bavasi, Alston was the strongest man on the team.

"Pee Wee told me that on one bus trip, some of the players were complaining about the ride," said Bavasi. "Walter stopped the bus, got out of his seat, and said that anyone who [didn't] like the bus [could] 'get out right now before I throw you out. And that goes for you too, Frank Howard.' And Howard was a giant of a man, 6'7" and about 260 pounds. Alston had made his point."

> Bavasi brought Alston to the major leagues and Alston stayed for 23 years, outlasting Bavasi with the Dodgers, and was elected to the Hall of Fame. That is Buzzie Bavasi's lasting legacy to the Dodgers, and to baseball. "Walter Alston was my man," Bavasi said. "I loved him."

That headline perfectly sums up the reaction of Dodgers fans and players, and of baseball people in general, to the choice. Although a few Dodgers had played for him in the minor leagues, I didn't know him, and most people had no idea who he was. He had come out of Miami University (Ohio) to play minor league baseball for 13 seasons. He reached the major leagues with the St. Louis Cardinals in 1936, batted once, struck out, and was never heard from again.

Alston began his managerial career in 1940 as player/manager for Portsmouth in the Mid-Atlantic League but was hardly a success as either a player or a manager. Three years later, Dodgers president Branch Rickey, who had known Alston when Rickey was general manager of the Cardinals, hired Alston as player/manager of Trenton in the Interstate League. That began a 10-year run for Alston as a manager in the Dodgers' minor league system, in which he eventually rose to the farm team in Montreal.

Alston wasn't a very good manager in 1954, his first year with the Dodgers. He took a veteran team with a lot of stars that had won two straight pennants and finished second, five games behind the Giants. I think it was a combination of things that worked against Alston that first year. He might have been intimidated by all the great players around him. As players we had no respect for this rookie manager who had no major league pedigree as either a player or manager.

Alston and Jackie Robinson never hit it off. Don't get the idea that it was a racial thing. I never got the sense that Alston was racist. In fact, Alston had Roy Campanella and Don Newcombe in their first year of professional ball at Nashua and got along well with both of them, and he loved Jim Gilliam. He even made Gilliam a coach, a position Jim held for 12 years under Alston. And Walter flat-out bawled giving the eulogy at Gilliam's funeral in 1978. It was the only time I ever saw Alston cry.

But there was something Jackie didn't like about Alston. I never found out what it was. One thing I do remember, though, is that Jackie had been injured and missed a few games, and he mentioned to the media that he was ready to play and Alston wouldn't play him. That comment got into the papers, and in a clubhouse meeting, Walter confronted Jackie, and the two of them almost got into a fight. It would have been a good one. Alston was a pretty strong, powerful man, about 6'2" and 200 pounds. And Jackie could fight.

Another time, Jackie was called out in a close play at second base. He argued long and loud with the umpire, but Alston never left the dugout to take up the fight for Robinson, which managers, whether they believe the umpire blew the call or not, are expected to do for two reasons: to show their support for their players and to make certain the player doesn't get thrown out of the game. Whether or not Alston didn't move because he wanted to show Robinson up, I don't know. What I do know is that Jackie was angry that his manager wouldn't go out there and fight for him.

With a year under his belt, Alston became a better manager. We won the pennant and Brooklyn's only World Series in 1955. But Walter really became a good manager when we went to Los Angeles, once he was rid of the Brooklyn element—the veteran players who were there when he arrived—and was able to bring in his own players. He learned to adjust to his personnel. When he had a team with great pitching and very little offense, he'd bunt in the first inning, steal a base, and score a run without a hit, things like that. He learned how to manufacture runs, and he became a Hall of Fame manager.

Alston was an organization's manager; he never asked for a multiyear contract, as Dressen did, and he never got one. But he did sign 23 one-year contracts, and in those 23 years he won seven pennants and four world championships.

I played for **Leo Durocher** for only half a season—73 games in 1948—but half a season was enough for me to get a pretty good line on Durocher's personality, warts and all. Leo was arrogant, egotistical, abrasive, profane, and ruthless. He would do anything to win, and I mean *anything*—steal signs, order his pitchers to throw at hitters ("Stick it in his ear!" he'd yell from the dugout. "Let's see how he hits flat on his back."), ride opposing players relentlessly from the bench, and continually torment umpires by running out and arguing calls at the drop of a hat. That's why he was known as "Leo the Lip."

But he was also a brilliant baseball strategist, very creative and innovative, and one of the most colorful characters in the history of baseball. He had a way of getting the most out of his players, usually by goading and demeaning them.

Manager Leo Durocher (left) shows why he was nicknamed "the Lip" as he engages in a conversation with umpire George Magerkurth during a 1946 game.

Durocher had been a good-fielding, no-hit shortstop in the big leagues for 17 seasons, playing with the Yankees, the Reds, the famed Cardinals Gashouse Gang (the perfect marriage of temperaments between player and team), and later the Dodgers, who traded four players to bring Leo to Brooklyn after the 1937 season.

On the field, Leo would cut his opponents' throats. I respected him, even as an opponent, because when the game started, he was out there to win—no matter what. If he had to cheat a little bit, he'd cheat. Steal signs? He'd steal signs.

To his credit, Dodgers president Larry MacPhail recognized Durocher's leadership ability and made him player/manager in 1939. Almost immediately, Durocher transformed a mediocre team into a contender in the National League. He had the good baseball smarts to turn his shortstop job over to Pee Wee Reese in 1940, recognizing that Pee Wee was someone around whom he could build a team. Later it was Durocher who converted Gil Hodges from catcher to first baseman, giving the catching job to Roy Campanella.

Perhaps Durocher's finest moment was when he stood in full support of Jackie Robinson and put down the attempted rebellion of those players who voiced their opposition to playing with a black man. And when the Dodgers won the pennant in 1941, it was their first championship in 21 years, and Durocher became a hero in Brooklyn, hailed as a great leader.

Leo's undoing in Brooklyn came when his flamboyant lifestyle caught up with him. He liked to associate with unsavory characters, and in 1947 commissioner Happy Chandler shocked the baseball world and devastated the borough of Brooklyn by suspending Durocher for one year for conduct "detrimental to baseball." Leo had allegedly consorted with known gamblers.

Durocher returned to the Dodgers in 1948, my second season. When we fell into fourth place in July, the Dodgers fired Leo and brought back Burt Shotton, who had managed the team to a pennant the year Durocher was under suspension. At just about that time, the Giants fired their manager, Mel Ott, and shocked the baseball world by hiring Durocher to replace him. So Leo, who had been vicious in his attacks on the Giants when he managed the Dodgers, was now the manager of the hated Giants, and he turned his venom on us.

Durocher was an interesting and complex individual. Off the field, he could charm you to death. He was a fancy dresser who liked to hang around people in show business. He was married to movie star Larraine Day, a beautiful and classy woman. On the field, Leo would cut his opponents' throats. I respected him, even as an opponent, because when the game started, he was out there to win—no matter what. If he had to cheat a little bit, he'd cheat. Steal signs? He'd steal signs.

The story that the Giants stole signs in the Polo Grounds in the third game of the 1951 playoff doesn't surprise me. It could all be true. I don't know for a fact that it was true, but it wouldn't surprise me because Leo was the manager. But I have to wonder, if the Giants were getting our signs, how did Don Newcombe strike out three in a row the inning before Bobby Thomson hit his home run? And why did it take until the ninth inning for the Giants to take advantage of getting our signs? Why did they wait so long?

Even if the Giants did have our signs, there's nothing in the rules book against it so long as they were getting the signs without using cameras or other illegal devices. I had signs given to me by Reese when he was on second base and could see the catcher's signs. There's nothing illegal about that. That's part of the game. It's like the steroid issue. A player can use illegal drugs to get stronger and a player can get signs from a teammate, but he still has to hit the ball. That's what Barry Bonds said, and I agree with him 100 percent. No matter how strong a player gets, he still has to hit the ball. And even if he got our signs, Bobby Thomson still had to hit the ball that October afternoon in 1951. And Bobby Thomson hit the ball.

When that happened and we watched Leo in the third-base coach's box, slapping Thomson on the rear end as he rounded third base, hugging Eddie Stanky, going crazy, it all came into focus for me—all the reasons you loved Leo when he was your manager and hated him when he was your opponent's manager.

Tommy Lasorda and I were teammates briefly with the Brooklyn Dodgers in 1954 and 1955, but maybe the less said about Tommy's playing career, the better. He was a left-handed pitcher who appeared in eight games for the Dodgers, a total of 13 innings, without winning a game or losing one.

Tommy Lasorda the manager is a different story. He was the perfect manager for a team so close to Hollywood. Lasorda was, and is, very theatrical. He loved to be in the company of stars, like Frank Sinatra, Dean Martin, Don Rickles, and Milton Berle. The fans loved him, and he was a favorite of writers' with his jokes and one-liners, hugging his players after they hit home

Manager Tommy Lasorda rushes out to congratulate Derrel Thomas after Thomas scored a pivotal run during the 1981 World Series.

runs, and telling people that he bleeds Dodger Blue. He's a terrific after-dinner speaker and has become something of a baseball ambassador.

Tommy has a million stories—I think he stays up at night thinking of them. One that I have heard him tell many times at banquets is that his wife would get frustrated with him because he was always talking about baseball.

The fans loved [Lasorda], and he was a favorite of writers' with his jokes and one-liners, hugging his players after they hit home runs, and telling people that he bleeds Dodger Blue.

"Tommy," she supposedly said, "sometimes I think you love baseball more than you love me."

And Tommy is supposed to have replied, "Yeah, but I love you more than I love basketball and football."

For all his bluster, Tommy was a very successful manager. He managed the Dodgers for 3,041 games and 21 seasons. Only Walter Alston, with 3,657 games and 23 seasons, managed the Dodgers longer. Tommy won 1,599 games, had a winning percentage of .526, and won five pennants and three World Series.

So popular was **Wilbert Robinson** in Brooklyn—they called him Uncle Robbie—that in the years he managed the Dodgers, from 1914 to 1931, the team was called the Robins.

Robinson had been an outstanding catcher for the old Baltimore Orioles before the turn of the 20th century. He was known mostly for his defense, his baseball intelligence, and his durability (he caught more than 1,300 games in a 17-year career and once was behind the plate for five games in two days).

While with the Orioles, Robinson was a teammate and close friend of John McGraw, the legendary "Little Napoleon," who managed the New York Giants for 31 years and won 2,763 games, more than any manager in baseball history except Connie Mack. In their playing days, Robinson and McGraw were inseparable. They even became partners in a thriving Baltimore billiards parlor and saloon, despite their diverse personalities—McGraw was a hard-driving, demanding, abrasive martinet and Robinson an easygoing, laid-back, avuncular charmer.

Wilbert Robinson's status in Brooklyn caused the team to be known as the Robins while he was in charge.

When McGraw took over as manager of the Giants in 1902, he brought his pal Robinson with him as pitching coach. The two worked hand-in-hand for 11 years, but in 1913 the close friends had a falling out over something silly and simple—a missed sign.

With the Brooklyn club in a state of turmoil (they hadn't finished higher than fifth in 11 consecutive seasons) and seeking a new manager, the popular Robinson, a favorite among New York's sportswriters, was the obvious choice. He was hired as Brooklyn's manager in 1914. Two years later he drove Brooklyn to its first pennant in 16 years.

Robinson's managerial style was the antithesis of McGraw's. While McGraw ran the Giants with an iron fist, Robinson handled the Brooklyn team with kid gloves, coaxing major contributions out of aging players like Rube Marquard, Dazzy Vance, Jake Daubert, and Zack Wheat. When he won the National League pennant again in 1920, Robinson was forever enshrined in the pantheon of Brooklyn baseball heroes and was rewarded for his contribution with partial ownership and the title of team president.

In 1932, two years before his death, Uncle Robbie was replaced as manager of the Dodgers by Max Carey. Although his record as manager was only slightly above .500 (1,399–1,398), his legacy was secure—so was his contribution to the zaniness that marked the Dodgers throughout their history.

One spring, Robinson boasted that he would outdo a famous stunt by Washington catcher Gabby Street, who gained a measure of fame by catching a baseball dropped from the top of the Washington Monument. Robbie arranged to catch a ball dropped from an airplane.

The stunt was set up, and on the fateful day, Robinson poised beneath the plane and waited for the projectile to fall. Down it came as Robinson circled underneath. The missile plopped into Robinson's mitt and exploded on impact. With his eyes shut and his chest covered with moisture, Robinson thought he had been covered with blood, until he heard the raucous laughter of his teammates.

Someone had substituted a grapefruit for the baseball. That someone, it will come as no surprise, is believed to have been the mischievous prankster Casey Stengel.

Statistical Summaries

All statistics are for manager's Dodgers career only.

MANAGING

G = Games managed

W = Games won

L = Games lost

PCT = Winning percentage

P = Pennants

WS = World Series victories

Manager	Years	G	W	L	PCT	P	WS
Charlie Dressen *First manager to take Dodgers to consecutive World Series*	1951–53	468	298	166	.642	2	0
Walter Alston *Winning manager in a record seven All-Star Games, with an overall record of 7–1*	1954–76	3,658	2,040	1,613	.558	7	4
Leo Durocher *Dodgers' last player/ manager*	1939–46 1948	1,318	738	565	.566	1	0

continued	Years	G	W	L	PCT	P	WS
Tommy Lasorda *First NL manager to win pennants each of his first two seasons*	1976–96	3,041	1,599	1,439	.526	4	2
Wilbert Robinson *Dodgers played 19 tie games during his 19 seasons*	1914–31	2,736	1,375	1,341	.506	2	0

Index

Entries in italics denote references to photo captions.

ROY CAMPANELLA • JOHN ROSEBORO • STEVE YE.
CAMILLI • STEVE GARVEY • WES PARKER • EDDIE MU
BILLY HERMAN • EDDIE STANKY • PEE WEE REESE •
FREY • ARKY VAUGHAN • BILLY COX • RON CEY • CC
WHEAT • AUGIE GALAN • LOU JOHNSON • PETE REISE
CAREY • CARL FURILLO • REGGIE SMITH • DIXIE WAL
• DON NEWCOMBE • DAZZY VANCE • BURLEIGH C
ROE • JOHNNY PODRES • FERNANDO VALENZUEL/
PERRANOSKI • HUGH CASEY • ED ROEBUCK • CHA
WILBERT ROBINSON • ROY CAMPANELLA • JOHN RO
HODGES • DOLPH CAMILLI • STEVE GARVEY • WES PAR
DAVEY LOPES • BILLY HERMAN • EDDIE STANKY •
DUROCHER • LONNY FREY • ARKY VAUGHAN • BILLY
TOMMY DAVIS • ZACK WHEAT • AUGIE GALAN • LOU J(
RICK MONDAY • MAX CAREY • CARL FURILLO • RE
HOWARD • DON DRYSDALE • DON NEWCOMBE • DAZ.
KOUFAX • PREACHER ROE • JOHNNY PODRES • FERNA
LABINE • RON PERRANOSKI • HUGH CASEY • ED ROE
LASORDA • WILBERT ROBINSON • ROY CAMPANELLA